DETECTIVE STORIES
FROM THE BIBLE

Detective Stories from the Bible

J. Ellsworth Kalas

Abingdon Press
Nashville

DETECTIVE STORIES FROM THE BIBLE

Library of Congress Cataloging-in-Publication Data

Kalas, J. Ellsworth, 1923-
  Detective stories from the Bible / J. Ellsworth Kalas.
    p. cm.
  ISBN 978-1-4267-0256-3 (pbk. : alk. paper)
    1. Bible—Criticism, interpretation, etc. 2. Bible stories. 3. True crime stories.
I. Title.
  BS511.3.K35 2009
  220.6'1—dc22

                                                            2009017552

09 10 11 12 13 14 15 16 17 18 — 10 9 8 7 6 5 4 3 2 1

MANUFACTURED IN THE UNITED STATES OF AMERICA

*To the members of my Asbury
Seminary Cabinet:*

Leslie Andrews   *Bryan Blankenship*
Steve Harper   *Ronnie Jones*
Sheila Lovell   *Hugo Magallanes*
Tapiwa Mucherera *Bill Tillman*
John David Walt

*Your friendship, dedication, and faithful
labors blessed and strengthened my years
in a challenging assignment.*

CONTENTS

FOREWORD

For years I have been fascinated that several of England's most celebrated mystery writers were also very popular (though not professional) Christian theologians. One thinks especially of G. K. Chesterton and Dorothy Sayers. I asked myself what these rather different careers and interests had in common.

There's probably a complex answer, one that might call for a psychological or philosophical treatise. I'm satisfied to conclude simply that the Bible deals with any number of mysteries, so it's no wonder that thoughtful Christians who happened to write mystery stories would also write about theology.

After all, what could be more of a mystery than God's love for the human race? Why would God care so intensely about what happened to a particular species on one of the innumerable planets? And how is it that this planet, which on the one hand is so full of beauty and promise, should also have gotten into such a mess?

And then there's the man called Job: a quite admirable character whose whole life suddenly fell apart. When he got to the end of his whirlwind experience, what did he think about it all?

I was taken, too, with a man who began as an obscure middle child in a large, rather dysfunctional family—a man whose early career was marked by the most egregious kind of misconduct—but who along the way gave his name to what is in my judgment the most remarkable ethnic / religious group on our planet and who, when you come to the end of the biblical story, is the center of attention.

So that's what led to this book. These stories are not all mystery stories in the conventional sense of the word, but they investigate incidents, personalities, and topics that ought to catch the interest of anyone with a detective's turn of mind.

Enjoy, please, and learn. And especially, above all, get a new interest in the Bible and with that interest a new fascination with God, the grandest Mystery—the One who at the same time is quite beyond our wildest reach, yet always is soliciting our attention.

—J. Ellsworth Kalas

CHAPTER ONE

A BIOGRAPHY OF SATAN

When someone discovers a corpse and it's clear that the death is not by a natural cause, the trained inspector then determines if the death is by suicide or murder. If the signs point rather surely to a murder, the detective begins seeking clues that will lead to the perpetrator—or the *perp*, as crime writers and television cops like to say. The same rule applies to theft, assault, or those sometimes subtle violations of the law that we identify in that more sophisticated category called "white-collar" crimes: you know that *somebody* must have done it.

By the way, if you figure that white-collar crime (such a nice name, isn't it!) doesn't quite fit into our story because there's usually no blood at the crime scene, only a meticulous spreadsheet—well, let's just say that it's eerily appropriate that we refer to financial losses as "red ink." If your resources are wiped out, that red ink looks like blood flowing at the bottom of the page. And sometimes, as you know, it even *leads* to blood, whether in a murder or a suicide. (And while I'm thinking about it, it occurs to me that Jesus attacked what might be called "white-collar sins"— the thoughts and intents of our hearts—more than he did the more obvious sins. That's probably worth thinking about some more.)

Anyway, whatever the crime, we want to know who is responsible, because only then can we bring the perpetrator to justice. And also, not so incidentally, only then can we get the person off the streets before still more harm is done. Sometimes—perhaps even most of the time—the perpetrator moves from one victim to another. We have a term for it if the crime is murder: *serial killer*. And if the crime is fraud, sometimes the thief simply moves from one victim or community or industry to another, leaving behind a trail of broken people and bankrupt businesses.

There's no use in my trying to be subtle. You want me to get to the point. All of us know that something malevolent is loose in our world. And it's been this way for a long time. How long? Well, if it's murder we're talking about, the Bible would take us all the way back to the first family, where murder came to birth between siblings Cain and Abel. And if it's white-collar crime, you can go back almost as far to another family scene, where a younger brother, Jacob, swindled his older twin, Esau.

But when we look for the perpetrator, we slowly realize that the story is older than either of these crime scenes. Cain and Jacob are really pretty small potatoes. There's somebody more involved, because this is a much bigger deal than a murder here or a fraud there. There's something twisted right at the heart of things. All of us know it, and from as far back as we can imagine, the human race has known it and has sought a name for it. We know there's some master perpetrator, some evil genius at work beyond our imagining, a mind so conscientiously evil that we see evidences of his activity everywhere, in every part of the world, in every culture, and without regard for race, sex, age, or color.

We have a name for him—several names, in fact. *Satan. The devil. The serpent. Lucifer. Beelzebub. Belial.* In more recent times, *Mephistopheles.* And, of course, nicknames have developed too, because anybody as familiar as this character is tagged with names that make him more manageable, like *Old Nick* or *Old Scratch.* Which is to say, if we were to post a villain's description in a plan for apprehending, we'd have a long list of aliases. And of course I've stuck pretty much to the language of the biblical world and the Western world, and haven't even approached the names you'd find in some cultures of Africa, South America, Asia, or the islands of the sea. I suspect, however, that we'd find appropriate names in all of those places, with definitions basically not too different from our own.

As I see it the most descriptive name is the basic biblical term—*the adversary*. That is, the ultimate perpetrator; the one who really has it in for us; the one who wants most to discomfit, disrupt, disassemble, and destroy us. The adversary. The one so much against us that when passing adversaries appear on the scene, even so transient and unimportant as the person who crowds ahead of us in the checkout line, we figure the devil has had something to do with it. That's why we laughed so readily a generation ago when a comedian developed a character who always excused her conduct by saying, "The devil made me do it." The comedian made us feel better about the little acts of nastiness that seem to mark most of our lives at one time or another: we can say that somebody gave us a push. The language gives an almost cozy, playful quality to the villain.

And "villain" is of course the right description. The human story is so ideal, almost impossibly so, until this villain appears. The man and the woman—let's call them Adam and Eve—are so happy that the man says, "At last! This is what I've been waiting for: bone of my bones and flesh of my flesh" (Genesis 2:23, paraphrased). They're both naked, but they're so comfortable with themselves, with each other, and with their total environment (we call it *Eden: paradise*) that there's no shame. Shame is something you feel only if you're uncomfortable for some reason or other, and there was nothing here to destroy comfort.

But then came the villain. He didn't look it. But the writer tells us, flat out, that he is "more crafty than any other wild animal that the LORD God had made" (Genesis

3:1). He's so crafty, in fact, that—well, you've heard the old line about the salesman who could sell refrigerators to people in the Arctic? This character moved into perfection and convinced the man and the woman that he had something that would improve on perfection—something heretofore lacking, so that the persuasive villain's offer would put all other wonders in the shade. He put up one small minus sign that made all the pluses of paradise seem a deficit.

The writer of Genesis doesn't give this villain a name. The writer simply refers to him as "the serpent." But when we get to the end of the story—or perhaps I should say, to the beginning of the endless-end of the story—the writer of Revelation picks up the same name. He calls this villain "the dragon, *that ancient serpent,* who is the Devil and Satan" (Revelation 20:2, italics added).

But I'm not intending to give anything away by hurrying you to the end. While there's something very comforting about the end, we're still dealing with the perpetrator right now, and it seems clear that we'll have to do so as long as this earth is in its present state. So let's pick up the story where we left off.

After Adam and Eve bought the serpent's offer, they lost their home. They were left with zilch. Not only were they put out of their home, they were put out of the whole lovely Eden, and the door was locked so they'd never get in again. The only thing they had left, which they conveniently passed on to us, was a memory of what life in Eden had been like. Thus we humans keep thinking things should be better than they are, and we keep dreaming about levels of happiness that no one has ever experienced—at least not for more than a fleeting moment—but that we somehow think must be possible. And worse, it is a perfection that we want to pursue, because the instinct for such happiness is somewhere in our souls, a lost chord that some inner ear keeps trying to identify.

Now here's a predicament. We're introduced early to this disturber of our tranquillity, after which he seems to go underground—though there's continuing evidence of his activity. We have a murder as the story unfolds: the older son in this infamous first family (Cain) kills his younger brother (Abel). But there's no mention of the serpent. You get the feeling that, having posted some ineradicable venom in the human race, the serpent can now slide along his way exercising little effort of his own because humans are doing the job for him. It gets so bad, in fact, that the epic historian says that "the wickedness of humankind was great in the earth, and that every inclination of the thoughts of their hearts was only evil continually" (Genesis 6:5).

Mind you, goodness kept reasserting itself, no matter how rampant the odds against goodness. But here's the rub: even the residents of virtue are not immune to the evil that has been let loose. So Noah, a perfect man in his generation, is hardly off his redemptive voyage before he humiliates himself in a drunken stupor. And Abraham, the repository of hope, lies about his beloved Sarah, putting her in danger. And Jacob, one whom God seemed especially to bless, cheats his brother and deceives his father.

But I'm getting ahead of my story, because you want to know how this serpent, this villain—the one we call the Adversary—you want to know where he (or it) got its start.

If possible, I'd just as soon not get into this part of the story, because it's all so speculative. But I have no right to skirt the subject. I like the language of that seventeenth-century detective John Milton: ". . . what time his pride / Had cast him out from Heaven, with all his host / Of rebel Angels, by whose aid aspiring / To set himself in glory above his peers, / He trusted to have equaled the Most High."[1] In brief, Milton saw the Adversary as a creature who had once been part of the heavenly host but whose pride caused him to organize a group of rebel angels, expecting someday "to have equaled the Most High."

Milton had built his idea around the insights of a much earlier detective, the prophet Isaiah. Isaiah speaks of the "Day Star, son of Dawn" who had "fallen from heaven" after saying, "I will ascend to heaven; . . . I will make myself like the Most High" (Isaiah 14:12-14). And Milton no doubt found help in some other able early detectives—like Origen (A.D. 185–254), Jerome (ca. A.D. 347–420), and Augustine (A.D. 354–430) to name just a few. Augustine acknowledged that Isaiah was speaking of the King of Babylon, but that "of course" those references were "to be understood of the devil."[2]

Now of course you find this rather vague. You want a sharper description of the perpetrator, and because he seems to be a criminal hardened beyond change with a record that stretches across all of human history, you want to know what made him like this. And since such hard data is lacking, we tend to resort to language that obfuscates rather than reveals. That's what another pretty good detective, novelist Flannery O'Connor, warned against. "Our salvation," she wrote to John Hawkes (November 20, 1959) "is played out with the Devil, a Devil who is not simply generalized evil, but an evil intelligence determined on its own supremacy."[3]

Madeleine L'Engle offers a similar clue: "Evil is not simply the absence of good, as some say, but a positive force for evil. It is trying to snuff out the light."[4] She points out that Lucifer, who was meant to be a light-bearer, became instead the source of all evil because he wanted to be the light. And Kathleen Norris, that sensitive observer of our contemporary scene, reminds us that this malevolence invades even sacred places. "Evil is real," she writes, "and not theoretical. Scratch the surface of any ordinary church congregation and you will find not hypocrites but people struggling with demons."[5]

But let's turn to the ultimate authority on the Adversary, the One so opposite in nature that he could read Satan's nature with utter clarity. Listen: "He [Satan] was a murderer from the beginning and does not stand in the truth, because there is no truth in him. When he lies, he speaks according to his own nature, for he is a liar and the father of lies" (John 8:44). Tough language, especially coming from Jesus. Jesus made the point in a story about a landholder who sowed good grain in his field, "but while everybody was asleep, an enemy came and sowed weeds among the wheat." When the corrupted field revealed itself, the owner's workers asked how such a thing could have happened. The landowner replied, "An enemy has done this" (Matthew 13:24-30). *Enemy* is the right word. Martin Luther, in the hymn for which he is best known, "A Mighty Fortress Is Our God," referred to Satan as "our ancient foe" who "seek(s) to work us woe." So Rowan Williams, the Archbishop of Canterbury, warns against thinking of the devil as "a convenient metaphor for extreme wickedness" or "a kind of symbol" or an "externalization of inner conflicts." He is "not a symbol from our conscious imaginings, but something that waits for us."[6]

I pause too at Jesus' story of a farmer who is sowing seed. Some of the seed (which, Jesus explains, represents the word of the kingdom) falls on the pathway, and almost immediately "the evil one comes and snatches away what is sown in the heart" (Matthew 13:19). This is the primary business of "the evil one," to prevent us humans from accepting the redeeming message. Since he is the "father of lies," nothing disturbs him more than the prospect of our getting the truth. Most of us recognize the Adversary best when he comes in the form of disaster or trouble or pain. But for our Adversary, these are only means to an end. The goal of the Adversary is to keep us from truth. Because, of course, the ultimate goal of our enemy is to keep *us*. The truth will set us free. We must therefore, by all means, be kept from the truth.

Three of the Gospels tell us of Jesus' particular encounter with the Adversary, and Luke—whose report is the longest—concludes by saying that the devil "departed from him until an opportune time" (Luke 4:13). As I read the gospel stories about Jesus, I suspect that there were "opportune times" without end. In my mind, the most instructive element in this story is in the very fact that the Adversary dared to approach Jesus, and did so repeatedly. Here we have a measure of the arrogance of our enemy and of his unceasing ambition. Having lost his place in the heavenlies because of his prideful rebellion (as Isaiah and his interpreters tell the story) but having then succeeded in ruining Eden and setting up a beachhead on all human souls, the Adversary obviously saw no reason he could not also seduce God's Son, now that the Son was made vulnerable by inhabiting human flesh.

If the Adversary is so arrogant as to approach Jesus, we shouldn't be surprised that he constantly harasses *us*. After all, each time the Adversary wins some measure of victory in your life or mine, he has mocked the sacrifice of our Lord at Calvary. I suspect that the greatest saints are those persons who are most sensitive to the fact that they have an enemy and that they have the power from Christ to cope with that enemy. But they have also learned that they need help in dealing with this Adversary.

This is a sharply abbreviated biography. There's so much more that could be written. The documents from any given day on our planet would pack solid the average county courthouse. The Adversary's crimes range all the way from murder and betrayal and incest and child abuse—the evils that we most easily abhor—to ennui (such a subtle foe!) and normal greed ("I've got my rights," we say) and arrogance and unseemly pride. And of course we have to remember that all of us find it nearly impossible to tell the difference between *seemly* and *unseemly* pride. That's why the great Augustine—who knew a good deal by experience about sin—insisted that "pride is the beginning of all sin."

I should tell you that this Ultimate Perpetrator will eventually be apprehended. Justice will be done. The report was so real to the writer of Revelation that he tells it as something already done: "the devil" (John notes again that he is a deceiver) is "thrown into the lake of fire and sulfur, where the beast and the false prophet were, and they will be tormented day and night forever and ever" (Revelation 20:10). Incidentally, I'm glad that the book of Revelation ends not on this graphic note of destruction but with a description of the beauties of the new heaven and the new earth, and God's invitation to "everyone who is thirsty" to come (Revelation 22:17).

I mentioned earlier that one of the aims of our criminal system is to get the repeat offender off the streets, to protect the larger population. So what hope does our planet have regarding this age-long enemy? Let's face it: this Adversary is helpless without our cooperation. He struts and swaggers and smiles condescendingly on our struggling race, but he's really quite helpless except as we help him. Until our Lord gives the final victory, the best thing you and I can do is get this offender off the streets of our own souls. If enough of us would do so, we'd be surprised at what a difference it would make on our whole planet.

CHAPTER TWO

FOLLOW THE BLOOD

E ven a rookie newspaper reporter, new to the police beat, knows that if there is blood at the scene of a crime, you'd better follow it. And when you see where the blood leads, you can begin putting together the rest of the story until at last all the pieces are in place. At that point, you may have the conclusion you expected or you may have a conclusion that surprises you.

So follow me, please, while I take you to a place of blood. I'm not a newspaper reporter, but I've worked this particular beat for five decades or more, so it is familiar territory to me. That is, I am an ordained minister of a Christian denomination, so I encounter blood frequently. If I were a member of an Episcopal, an Anglican, a Lutheran, or a Disciples of Christ congregation, this meeting with blood could be a weekly affair; and if I were a particularly devout Roman Catholic—that is, one who attends Mass regularly—the occasion might be daily.

That's because blood is part of the ritual of most Christian bodies. I dare to say that it is a *routine* part, in that perhaps a majority of worshipers hardly give the matter a second thought. It's surprising that we don't follow this trail of blood that we encounter so often. For some of us, I suspect it's because if we've grown up in a church we take the traditional practices for granted. For others, the ritual is so sacred that it seems improper to ask questions.

But try for a moment to imagine yourself a stranger to Christian practices: doesn't something about our communion service strike you as odd? You come to a meeting place to worship Almighty God, and at some point the person leading the ritual says, "This is the body of Christ. Eat it." And then, "This is the blood of Christ. Drink it." In some of the early generations of the Christian faith, when the movement was small and made up almost entirely of people without wealth or position, those who watched from afar overheard this Christian celebration and concluded that their neighbors must be cannibals. They seemed honorable enough in daily conduct; indeed, they were severe in their morality and integrity. But when they came together to worship, they talked of eating a body and drinking the blood. A strange people, indeed!

So let's follow this trail of blood. Pause as you leave the orderly, perhaps beautifully carved table with its linen cloths and its aesthetically appealing appointments and ask yourself how this all happened to be. How is it that such an unlikely celebration should be seen as the high point of Christian worship for hundreds of millions of people?

It's a very long story. Some parts are recorded for us in the Bible and in ancient sermons and rituals of the church. But we gain further understanding of the story by looking deep into our humanness, especially those elements of life so deeply embedded in us that we see them as instinctual.

The trail of blood begins dramatically and yet enigmatically when the writer of Genesis tells the story of the first murder, the assassination of Abel by his brother Cain. When God confronts Cain about what he has done, blood is the issue: "Listen; your brother's blood is crying out to me from the ground!" Still more: God tells Cain that the ground "has opened its mouth to receive your brother's blood from your hand" (Genesis 4:10-11).

I dare submit that every murder mystery ultimately draws its inspiration from this message to Cain: something about our human blood is so special that it cries out—not simply to the courts or to avengers but to Almighty God. And further, something about this blood is so uniquely significant that the very ground of creation is appalled by it, yet opens up to receive it. It is not simply that someone has died; it is that *blood* has been shed.

It's no wonder that primitive peoples involved blood with their religion. After all, if life was in the blood, then the best thing a person could give to whatever god they worshiped would involve blood. The primitive person may not have known much about the god or gods they worshiped, but they took their gods seriously, so they reasoned quite logically that the best way to demonstrate that they were in earnest was to offer a symbol of life—and the most logical way to do so was to give their god some blood.

The first such instance in the Bible followed the great Flood. As Noah and his family got off the ark, Noah built an altar to the Lord and took one of every clean animal and of every clean bird to make a sacrifice to God. This was an act of thanksgiving; it was not so much a plea for mercy as Noah's expression of gratitude that he and his family had survived.

And the shedding of blood was the most sensible and the most dramatic way to show this gratitude since blood is the essence and the symbol of life. When the blood goes, or when the heart ceases to beat so that the blood stops flowing, life ends. So the biblical writer says, almost matter-of-factly, "for the life of every creature is its blood" (Leviticus 17:14).

So it is that blood becomes a defining issue in the portion of the Bible that Judaism calls the Torah and that Christians call the Pentateuch or the Book of Moses. The book of Leviticus, which contains so many of the details of temple worship and of health regulations, mentions blood nearly ninety times. And those references that might seem to the casual reader as having to do simply with issues of health and sanitation actually have their source in matters of theology. That is, the extensive regulations around a woman's menstrual period find their significance in the fact that the blood represents life—in this case, blood that has not now consummated in life. It is the same concept that so frequently describes murder as the *shedding of blood,* because it finds in blood the very issue of life itself.

Here too is the reason for the prohibition against eating blood: "Only be strong not to eat the blood," the book of Deuteronomy commands, "for the blood is the life and you shall not eat the life in the meat."[1] And hear this. When the earliest Christian council had to decide if it would be proper to admit Gentiles into the faith (for the first Christians were all Jews by birth or conversion), the council had to decide what regulations of their heritage would be enforced on the new believers. The regulations were surprisingly few but included that they should "abstain . . . from blood" (Acts 15:20, 29).

The rituals of temple worship as outlined in the Old Testament books are replete with references to blood. Many seem peculiar to a twenty-first-century reader, but I suspect that this is because our sense of the sacredness of blood has diminished even while its medical importance has increased. For us, blood is classified by types and is complicated by references to platelets and plasma. In a sense, we understand blood so well that it has lost its mystery—and that's quite a loss. Because after we've taken blood apart in the laboratory, we're still left with the wonder that somewhere in the midst of those particles we are touching life itself. Our ancestors understood this element of the blood story, so while they were poorer than we are in their knowledge of science, they were richer in their sense of mystery. We know *more*; perhaps they knew *deeper*.

The heart of the matter was this. The people of Israel understood that death had come to the human race by way of sin. Since death was symbolized by the shedding of blood, the logical way to break the power that had caused death was to give a life—and blood symbolized life. Each time there was some use of blood in the act of worship it was a dramatic reenactment of the human predicament—a creature under the death penalty—and the divine remedy in the shedding or imposition of blood.

No wonder, then, that blood is so prominent in the Hebrew Scriptures. Where Christianity sees baptism as the symbol of admission to the holy community (the church), circumcision—with its shedding of blood—was the initiatory rite for the people of Israel. When Aaron, the first high priest of Israel, was ordained to his task, the blood of a ram was placed on his right earlobe, his right thumb, and his right big toe, and on that of his sons who were to follow him in spiritual leadership. Robert Alter notes that this ceremony symbolically touched on the organs of hearing, holding, and locomotion, thus indicating that they were dedicated wholly to their sacred task.[2]

Professor Alter acknowledges readily that the biblical reference to blood as a purifying agent "may strike the modern reader as . . . odd." He notes, however, that "throughout the Bible [and I assume that as a Hebrew scholar he is thinking of what Christians call the Old Testament, but I would note that the same theme continues in the New Testament] blood has powerfully antithetical valence, alternately identified as the stuff of life and the manifestation of guilt. Perhaps because it was thought to be the very bearer of the life force in animate creatures, it was understood to have what [Jacob] Milgrom vividly calls a 'detergent' effect."[3]

As Christianity came to birth, it moved beyond many of its Old Testament roots. Most crucially, as the Apostle Paul made clear, Christianity declared salvation not in the keeping of the Hebrew Law but in the grace revealed in Jesus Christ. But Christianity did not move beyond the message and the symbolism of blood; rather, it gave this message a whole new, more dramatic emphasis. Because now, in the New Testament, we are dealing not with the blood of lamb, ram, goat, or bull but the blood of Jesus Christ, the Son of

God. Thus Paul reminded his converts that the church was a body that God "obtained with the blood of his own Son" (Acts 20:28).

The New Testament Letter to the Hebrews (which speaks of blood even more often than the Old Testament book of Deuteronomy) builds on its Old Testament origins when it declares that "without the shedding of blood there is no forgiveness of sin" (Hebrews 9:22). But the power of the blood has taken on a whole new dimension. "And it is by God's will that we have been sanctified through the offering of the body of Jesus Christ once for all" (Hebrews 10:10). The blood ceremonies that were annual in ancient Judaism, and even more frequent in cases of individual repentance, were made complete, all-encompassing, and once-for-all in the death of Christ at Calvary.

So it is, then, that nearly all Christian churches celebrate this quite strange ceremony variously referred to as Holy Communion, the Sacrament, or Eucharist. This is our way of commemorating what our Lord did at Calvary. It is a trail of blood that begins in what was probably a universal sense of the sacredness of blood as recognized intuitively by ancient peoples as they sensed that life was, indeed, in this strange, interior substance, and that for biblical faith began with a declaration of blood's sacredness in Cain's murder of his brother Abel, and in its ritual celebration beginning with Noah and institutionalized with almost shocking detail in the books of Exodus, Leviticus, and Deuteronomy—and prominently in the prophet Ezekiel, and with breathtaking new significance in the New Testament.

But if we follow this trail of blood until we come to a contemporary place of worship—country church, massive cathedral, battlefield meeting of chaplain and troops—do we know what it means? Some find the whole idea repugnant, and though they may continue as church members they can't correctly refer to themselves as communicants because they avoid participating in this communion event.

And a vast number of other church members enter into this ceremony with little thought of the shocking picture that is spread before us in the celebration of Holy Communion.

The deeply pious in other generations accepted these references to the blood without uneasiness—rather, with profound affection. An unknown poet in the sixteenth or seventeenth century described the scene, though never specifically mentioning the blood:

> O sacred Head, now wounded,
> with grief and shame weighed down,
> now scornfully surrounded
> with thorns, thine only crown.[4]

Or Isaac Watts in 1707:

> Alas! and did my Savior bleed,
> and did my Sovereign die?

Or Charles Wesley, cofounder with his brother John of the Methodist movement in eighteenth-century England:

> Behold him, all ye that pass by,
> the bleeding Prince of life and peace!
> Come, sinners, see your Savior die,
> and say "Was ever grief like his?"
> Come, feel with me his blood applied:
> My Lord, my Love, is crucified.

Or that remarkable eighteenth-century poet William Cowper (1771):

> Dear dying Lamb, thy precious blood
> shall never lose its power
> till all the ransomed church of God
> be saved, to sin no more.

Or the stark simplicity of an African American spiritual, author unknown:

His blood came trickling down,
and he never said a mumbalin' word.

Or consider the words of one of the most revered devotional writers of the twentieth century, Thomas Merton. As a monk he had lived daily with the Psalms and had come to see some of their deeper significance. As Merton contemplated Psalm 21, he urged his readers to "unite ourselves with the dying Savior on the Cross, bury our sorrows in His pierced Heart, and feel our sins washed away by the saving tide of His Most Precious Blood."[5]

But without a doubt the language of the blood offends some modern sensibilities. I suspect that Kathleen Norris, that devout but quite urbane poet and essayist, may be right when she says, "As blood has gained in entertainment value in our culture, it has lost much of its religious significance." But she goes on to remind us that "both Judaism and Christianity are blood religions." More than that, she notes what may make some quite uneasy, that "the word 'bless' has its origins in blood." And then, with what I see as a wry smile, Ms. Norris writes, "That there is indeed 'Power in the Blood' can be demonstrated by the way in which the metaphor makes mainstream Protestants squirm."[6]

When a concept has lived for thousands of years—beginning for Jews and Christians in the earliest stories, rituals, and commandments of the Hebrew Scriptures and taking on poignant new significance for Christians in the death of Christ—I submit that the burden of acceptance is on the twenty-first-century inquirer to understand the concept rather than for the concept to accommodate itself to the peculiar and transient tastes of the current generation.

Let me put it baldly. If I am offended by the blood of worship, I should surely be offended by the medical use of transfusion. The principle is quite to the point. If I am at a point of life and death, I gratefully accept the blood of another human being, and I am particularly grateful that he or she is of the same blood type. I remember giving blood to one of my sisters many years ago as she awaited surgery. In that instance, the blood was taken directly from my body and given to hers. Neither she nor I found this exchange, or the hospital paraphernalia that expedited the process, offensive. I was glad, and so was she, that we could participate in claiming life through the blood.

Even so, since I take God seriously and since I take sin seriously—especially my sins!—I recognize that I am under a death penalty, and if death is involved I look for the blood remedy. As Fleming Rutledge, the Episcopal clergywoman, puts it, "The blood of Christ, Paul declares, has accomplished something that has changed the course of history and the direction of the universe. God did this."[7] I rejoice profoundly that there is a remedy, and even the delivery system through the church does not trouble me overmuch. I am simply glad that there is a way out of my predicament and that God has provided it.

Oh, yes, one other point. In the conventional mystery, we follow the blood to find out who is responsible for the death. In the biblical mystery, we follow the blood to find out who is responsible for the giving of *life*. And we trace the blood to the Christ of God at Calvary—a very bloody place, indeed. But it is the place where, by God's loving sacrifice, life is offered to our human race.

CHAPTER THREE

JOB TELLS HIS STORY

If you want a mystery story, I'll tell you a mystery story. Me. Job. All I ever really wanted was to please God. Some people want to be wealthy, probably especially because of the power that comes with land and money and ostentatious possessions. But wealth wasn't an issue for me, perhaps because it had always come rather easily for me—so easily that I suspect I didn't find the satisfaction in *getting* that stimulates most people. Others want prestige, community standing. I can't say that I didn't enjoy that sense of eminence; I'm sure I was gratified by the way people deferred to me, paying me those subtle and not-so-subtle acknowledgments that make one feel important. Some said I was the greatest man in the east, which is a rather large territory. But if I liked hearing such things, my good sense tempered my ego. I knew, for one thing, that if one has wealth a certain measure of standing comes with it. I'm also enough of a realist to know that public favor is ephemeral; it can disappear with the first snickering wind of ill.

Still others find their fulfillment in their family. Believe me, this was a major element in my life: my seven sons, my three daughters—they were like pieces of eternity in my soul. But I suspect that where for some an admirable family is a matter of social pride, for me they were a charge from God. My feeling for them found its determining core in my God-hunger so that day after day I rose early in the morning to offer a sacrifice to God for each of my children, fearing that perhaps in some inopportune moment one of them might have sinned against God—not by an egregious outward act but by a rebellious inward thought known to God alone. No doubt I was projecting onto my children the passion of my own unceasing desire to be close to God—so close that I might in some ecstatic moment catch a breath of the eternal. I felt that just one moment of such closeness would be all a person could ask in a lifetime, however long my life might be.

But before I go further, let me explain why I'm telling my story. Someone has said that the best mysteries are most memorable not for the crime but for the characters. Well, you can't produce a more memorable character than God, who is the lead character in this story, though not necessarily the one with the most lines. As for the villain, the embodiment of evil, I never really saw him, but I surely felt the violence of his blows. I was, myself, the third lead character. Now if I were only myself, I might be a quite dull personality. But as my story goes on, you will put other names on me, names of people you have known or read about—or perhaps even yourself. I am a kind of microcosm of anyone who has ever raised the question of why some people suffer to a degree that seems utterly irrational.

So those are the characters, and you'll admit their importance. As for the crime—well, I can't describe it adequately, and I certainly can't point to the perpetrator. Of course, you know more about the story than I do, because you've been given some background data in your Bible and some after-the-game evaluations. Even so, I don't think you can do a satisfactory crime scene investigation. You can tell me why evil exists in our world, but you can't say why the pain falls so unevenly or how it is that destruction lays its slimy hand on one house instead of the next. Sometimes, yes, but not always.

But let me get back to my story, and as I do, I hope there will be more light for some of the stories you know. In spite of my great desire to know God, I'm not sure but that the favors of life that surrounded me clouded my vision of God. I knew well enough that it shouldn't be so. A person should so love God that nothing else in life can compete with the holy hunger. Still, what one has can distract from the contemplation of what one has not, especially when the missing element is so difficult to define and the present elements are so near and strong and insistent. And of course the more one has, the greater the possibility of distraction.

Then one day, a tsunami of disaster swept over my life in one crashing wave after another. The day began in rather idyllic fashion. My sons and daughters were celebrating in the home of my eldest son; they had reason to celebrate, of course, because their lives were circumscribed by comfort. But even as I pondered my good fortune, one of my servants came running, so distraught he was nearly incoherent: a team of Sabeans had carried off our oxen and donkeys, killing all the attending servants except the message-bearer. While his word was still burning in my ears, another servant reported that a fire had fallen from heaven, burning up all my sheep and all the shepherds who were with them except for this one who had escaped. Then, a third messenger came with the news that some Chaldeans had carried off my camels, killing all the servants except this harried survivor.

I've already said that my wealth came to me easily. I held it with a light grasp. The most unnerving element in these three disasters was the message of conveyance: always one servant survived to deliver the bad news, as if some malevolent director orchestrating the disaster of my life had set up a reporting system in a way that would bring me the most pain.

But nothing could have prepared me for what was next. An especially trusted servant who was attending on my children as they celebrated came to me, head covered with ashes to say that a storm had leveled their meeting place, killing all of my children in a single blow. I had lost the single most significant object of my prayers, the exquisite compelling that brought me each morning to the place of sacrifice. I turned to the God who had given me my children: if he allowed them now to be taken away, who was I to argue?

Yet it seemed to me on that day-become-night that the hand of God that formerly had blessed and sheltered me had now entered league with some adversary against me. Previously it seemed that the universe made sense, that if I did what was right the results would be beneficent. Nevertheless, as the day ended, logic bowed before faith. God was good—in that I was confident. And all I wanted, still, was to see God.

Time passed by. I cannot say how long it was because in such circumstances time is the servant of imagination and fear. Somewhere, sometime, sores began to break out on my body. All of me—the part of me where I stood, where I sat, where I thought—was nothing but sores. There was of course physical pain, but it was nothing compared with my emotional pain, springing from the disgust I felt with my appearance and my stench. I despised my own body.

At this point my wife—God have mercy on her soul!—became my unsought counselor. Moved by my suffering she urged me to curse God and die. She spoke in love, no doubt of that. Nevertheless I couldn't resist thinking that perhaps she was also finding my presence unbearable; if so, I blame her not. If I despised my stench of a body why shouldn't she? But whatever drove her so to advise me, I rebuked her counsel. Since God had treated me so generously for so long, how dare I complain now that evil was befalling me?

I have siblings, but they didn't come to see me. Children drew back from the sight of me—children whose fathers had often pointed me out as a citizen to be emulated. My servants, an extraordinarily loyal brood, carefully stayed out of sight. No matter; I wouldn't have known what to ask of them if they had hovered at my beck as in time past. I came to love the ugly solitude of an ash heap, where I could scrape my boils with a piece of broken pottery.

But then three friends came. No, it was four; it's just that the fourth followed far enough behind, respecting his elders, that he seemed almost not to be part of the company, though certainly he asserted himself later. For seven days my friends said not a word. Their silence was a poultice to my soul, drawing out measures of pain.

The silence was sweet to me, yet it was more than I could bear. I sensed that they saw me as being in the wrong, so I wanted to make my case before they began theirs. And of course as soon as I began speaking, these men could hardly wait to respond. I suppose I sound unkind; perhaps I would have followed their course if I had been in their place. Apparently we humans feel compelled to tell others why they're in trouble. It's so much easier to understand other people's predicaments than our own.

Logic was on their side, of course. When my life was nothing but prosperity and achievement, they had said I was blessed by God, so now that everything was going wrong, the same pattern of thinking suggested that I was under a curse. And they meant to be God's defenders (as if God needs such), so they announced that I deserved the evil that was coming my way.

They did it eloquently. These men—Eliphaz, Bildad, and Zophar—were learned men, self-assured and certain of their philosophical ground. Eliphaz began gently and graciously, but he soon came to his point: I had strengthened other people in trouble, so "now it has come to you," he said, how is it that I was "dismayed"? It was a fair question, but a cold one, far too reasonable for my unreasonable pain. I argued back, syllogism on syllogism. I had lost my wealth, my children, and my health, but I would not let these friends rob me of my honor and my integrity. And I told them of my unaltered belief in God. I said it boldly: "How happy is the one whom God reproves; / therefore do not despise the discipline of the Almighty."[1] Did my friends—groomed, composed, successful—did they believe in God, bathed in blessing? No more than I did!

But I couldn't consistently maintain such a posture. Because try as I would to believe, I was struggling. The worst of it—worse than the losses that so shattered my previous life—was this, that I felt as if God were far from me, unwilling to face me so that I might plead my cause. I pleaded with my friends—indeed, with God!—to understand that God "is not a mortal, as I am, / that I might answer him, / that we should come to trial together."[2] The distance between us that had once seemed part of God's very magnificence now seemed foreboding and rejecting. Some voice from somewhere tried to convince me that God was now my enemy. I, who had wanted God so much, felt now that God had no audience for me.

Sometimes my friends seemed more anxious to diminish me than to show me the way. Zophar said in one instance, "Should your babble put others to silence, / and when you mock, shall no one shame you?"[3] As I look back on those days I ask myself why my friends—learned men, seemingly possessed of insight—would attack not the problem, not the issue, not the logic, but my very person. This was all I had left, wrapped as it was in my putrifying flesh, and this they seemed set on taking from me. On one occasion I railed back, "Miserable comforters are you all."[4] I'm not proud of my reply, but neither am I ashamed.

With all of their words, and with all of my replies, the only explanation I got was one I could not accept: that I had done wrong and that all that had happened to me was just retribution. Believe me, I feel we should face up to what we are and what we have done. But to assume evil of which we're not guilty is not only a lie it is a kind of reverse pride, claiming more malice than the soul has earned. I reasoned, too, that there is justice in God; whatever I had done, the suffering that had now come upon me was surely disproportionate.

Elihu, the young man who had remained silent while his elders spoke, now made his case. He was impatient with me for justifying myself rather than God and with the older friends for providing no answers. He insisted that God had, in fact, answered me—in a dream, he said, or "in a vision of the night, / when deep sleep falls on mortals, / while they slumber on their beds, / then he opens their ears, / and terrifies them with warnings."[5] In this perhaps Elihu was right. Perhaps in my absorption with my pain and in the unutterable agony of my loneliness, God's wooing of my soul fell on a deaf heart.

I never tried to answer Elihu. By that time I may have reached such a place of physical, intellectual, and spiritual exhaustion that I had nothing to say. Or perhaps Elihu's torrent of words left no entryway for my answers. But more likely, it seems to me, Elihu was preparing the way for God. I had wanted above all to please God, to see God, to hear God's voice. And at last my time came.

God answered me out of the whirlwind. Bruised and broken as I was, I wanted desperately for the divine embrace. Instead the voice challenged me to be a man, to show character worthy of a human being. "Gird up your loins like a man," God said. "I will question you, and you shall declare to me."[6] And with that word, God took me on a trip of creation such as no person has ever known. Ah, perhaps I overspeak! I don't know what anyone else has experienced. I only know for sure that I set out on a tour beyond all of my imagining.

It was a fascinating trip, led by the Ultimate Artist through the galleries of creation. The opening scene put me in place: "Where were you when I laid the foundation of the earth? / Tell me, if you have understanding."[7] Sometimes God's questions were philosophical: "Who has put wisdom in the inward parts, / or given understanding to the mind?"[8] But again, God would turn playful: "Do you know when the mountain goats give birth? . . . Who has let the wild ass go free?"[9] I wasn't sure when God was teasing me, when challenging me, or when both. And at no time did God pause for an answer. Sometimes I felt that this whirlwind trip was for the divine amusement and that I was simply being taken along for the ride. But at such moments I always recognized God's profound love not only for me but for all our human race—indeed, for all of the grand and diverse creation. I was made to feel that God had nothing else to do than to answer my question, to quiet my heart, to show me by way of this inimitable tour that I had nothing, ultimately, to fear: that a God who could put together such a wild and wonderful creation as this could surely be trusted with my life and all its problems.

At one point I thought the trip was over, when God announced that anyone "who argues with God must respond." I stammered my new self-evaluation, that "I am of small account." But God directed me again to gird up my loins like a man, for what turned out to be a kind of *coda* of the trip.

When at last the journey was complete, I made my witness: "I had heard of you by the hearing of the ear, / but now my eye sees you; / therefore I despise myself, / and repent in dust and ashes."[10]

You know the end of my story. I got back all I had lost and more, even seeing my children to four generations. My latter days were blessed more than anything in the earlier, abundant years.

As for the crime and the characters, well—I still don't fully understand the crime, this reality of evil in our world. I don't know why I should have suffered more monumentally than most people do, but two facts inform me: on one hand, I also enjoyed more favor than other people do. And also, the measure of pain is in the experience of the victim. Who can know enough about other people's circumstances to classify their pain? Sometimes one person's hangnail is another person's major surgery.

But though this crime of evil is still somehow beyond my understanding or explaining, it does not bother me as it once did. And this is because of the characters in the drama. The villain? He baffles me still. Why should there be such a disposition toward destruction, toward pain? I don't understand this, but neither do I understand how I, myself, sometimes am my own worst enemy and why sometimes I willingly, irrationally bring pain to others.

As for God, I know he can be trusted. I came to know this not because of the wonders of creation that I experienced but because God chose to invest in me the time to answer my questions. The answer was not in God's answers but in God's caring.

And as for me, the third person in the drama, I am at peace. All I ever wanted was to please God and to see God. Somewhere between the ash heap of my misery and the splendor of my journey through God's creation, I saw God and I saw that God was pleased with me. And now I know that nothing else matters.

CHAPTER FOUR

THE ADVANTAGES OF FOURTH PLACE

That master detective Sherlock Holmes always advised poor Dr. Watson—and anyone else who would listen—that we should never disregard anything, no matter how trivial. If you want to get to the root of matters, there's no such thing as a trivial pursuit. A broken twig, a raised eyebrow, a scuffed shoe, an apparently casual word—any of these may be crucial.

In the story I'm about to tell, the trivial detail is the apparently casual word—or more correctly, a recurrent pattern of such words.

Of course if you're in the habit of reading the Bible carefully you've discovered the importance of words. You've noticed that in the Genesis story of creation the universe comes into existence not through an engineering feat but by the power of words; God spoke, and the process unfolded. Later, in the New Testament book of John, the Savior of the world is identified as "the Word." Words matter.

Please join me as we get acquainted with a long-ago man. His name is Judah. I want you to keep an eye on the way words are wound round his name as his story unfolds.

There's no hint at the outset that Judah will ever matter. In the structures of the ancient world—and still in much of the world today—if you hope to count, you should arrange to be the firstborn in your family. This gives you all sorts of benefits connected with family wealth and the good family name. If you can't be born first, keep some semblance of hope by coming in second. As the British would put it, if you can't be the heir, be the spare. After all, there's always a chance (though you don't like to mention it) that something could happen to the firstborn.

In order to introduce Judah I have to give you a little messy family background. Judah's father, Jacob (later to be known as Israel), had two wives, sisters. He hadn't planned it that way. He had fallen in love with a girl named Rachel, the younger daughter of his uncle Laban. The Bible says that Rachel was "graceful and beautiful," which apparently was Jacob's evaluation also. Jacob and his future father-in-law agreed that he would work seven years for Laban to get Rachel as his wife. The biblical writer reports that the seven years "seemed to [Jacob] but a few days because of the love he had for her" (Genesis 29:20).

On the wedding night, however, the father-in-law—a person given to sharp dealings—substituted his older daughter, Leah, in the wedding tent. She was of course heavily veiled and in the kind of nighttime darkness that most of us in a world of artificial light never experience, so Jacob didn't know until morning that he had been duped. Perhaps wedding wine also dulled Jacob's perception. In any event, Jacob was married to Leah, a woman who had never caught his eye and who now through no fault of her own became despised, because for Jacob she represented fraud. Laban said that after the wedding week Jacob could also have Rachel as his wife, but that he would need to work another seven years in payment.

You can see that poor Leah was off to a bad start. She had one blessing, however: "When the Lord saw that Leah was unloved, he opened her womb; but Rachel was barren" (29:31).

The next few lines of the story are poignant with rejection and loneliness. When Leah's first son was born, she named him Reuben, "[b]ecause the Lord has looked on my affliction." Soon there was a second son, whom she named Simeon: "Because the Lord has heard that I am hated, he has given me this son also." A third son she named Levi, with hope: "Now this time my husband will be joined to me, because I have borne him three sons." And then Judah—and here there is a note of divine victory, some deep peace if only temporary: Judah, she said, because "This time I will praise the Lord." A lonely human being, unfairly rejected, she is confident in God. So Judah has something in his favor, a touch of faith and grace in his birth even though he is running a poor fourth.

Judah's name speaks of praise to God. Mark this down as a small but possible clue. It doesn't sound like much, but as Sherlock Holmes insists, we should never disregard anything, no matter how apparently trivial.

Eight brothers follow Judah in the family. One of them, Joseph, is the designated star from birth because he is born from Rachel, the beloved. Meanwhile Judah's three older brothers disqualify themselves from their seniority positions by conduct that offends their father. But there's no reason to expect anything of Judah, and the author of Genesis doesn't suggest that he is moving up the hierarchical ladder.

Late one afternoon, however, we hear Judah's voice for the first time. Frankly, it isn't a good or impressive expression. But we pay attention to first speeches because authors often use them to reveal the character of a person. All the older sons except Joseph are tending Jacob's extensive herds, a journey by foot of perhaps several days from their home. Jacob sends Joseph to check up on his brothers so he can bring a report back home. As Joseph approaches the camp, his brothers see this as their opportunity to be rid of their arrogant younger brother; they will murder him and convince their father that he has been killed by a wild beast.

While the brothers are keeping Joseph in a pit prior to his execution, a caravan of traders comes by. Here it is that

Judah speaks up. "What profit is it if we kill our brother and conceal his blood? Come, let us sell him to the Ishmaelites, and not lay our hands on him, for he is our brother, our own flesh" (37:26).

That succinct speech invites speculation. Is Judah simply a very clever operator who knows how to develop a win-win situation? By selling their brother into slavery, the brothers won't have his blood on their hands, and in addition they will pick up a nice piece of money. Or is Judah good at heart, hoping to find a way to save Joseph ("our own flesh") by persuading his brothers that Joseph is worth more alive than dead? When you read Judah's speech, you pay your money and you make your choice; I'll leave the character vote to you.

But I can tell you this. Without knowing it, Judah is co-operating with the eternal plot. He's helping to get Joseph down to Egypt, something that is essential to the rest of the biblical story. Because in Egypt, Joseph will eventually end up in the court of Pharaoh and be able to bring his father and brothers—the whole family clan, in fact—to Egypt, where in turn they will eventually, unfortunately, become slaves. But through this slavery they will be shaped into a nation, a body that will by both force and choice isolate themselves into a singular people, the Israelites. So it's by way of Judah's counsel that, in time, the family gets where they need to be if the rest of the story is to unfold. I doubt that Judah was a genius in this crucial development, but it's significant that he is the key element, and his first speech is thus a plot connector. He may have acted unwittingly, but a great many of our heroes fumble their way into greatness, so we'll let Judah do so as well. Still, you don't have to be much of a private eye to see that something else has happened. Judah has dared to test the waters of leadership, and his counsel has been accepted. The fourth choice in the family hierarchy has spoken up, and the council has listened.

But we really aren't ready for what happens next. Watch closely. Genesis 37 closes thus: "Meanwhile the Midianites had sold him [Joseph] in Egypt to Potiphar, one of Pharaoh's officials, the captain of the guard." Chapter 39 begins, "Now Joseph was taken down to Egypt, and Potiphar, an officer of Pharaoh, the captain of the guard, an Egyptian, bought him from the Ishmaelites who had brought him down there."

That is, chapters 37 and 39 are giving us the Joseph story, which to all evidence is the main plot. In fact it's such a big story that the Nobel Prize–winning novelist and essayist Thomas Mann could write four novels around it. So what is chapter 38 about that it dares to interrupt the story line? It's the heart of the Judah story, and a quite infamous heart at that, in which Judah becomes a faux hero.

The writer says, "It happened at that time," and gives us a series of incidents that cover twenty or thirty years. The phrase, "it happened at that time," is a storytelling device to let us know of some activity that is important to the major story line—important enough that the writer is laying aside the main plot temporarily in order to give us this sidebar story.

Now I must warn you that this isn't a pretty story, and if you insist on unsullied heroes I'd better excuse you from the room for a while. But the Bible is a wonderfully honest book. It shows us again and again that God works with the stuff at hand, however imperfect it may be. Personally, I'm grateful for this biblical picture of God, since it holds out hope for me, and probably for you, too. It is a picture of grace—the kind of grace that can take a rubbish heap and make from it a prospect of Eden.

Here's the story. Judah marries, and he and his wife have three sons. The first son marries a girl named Tamar, but this son displeases God and dies without having an heir. The second son marries Tamar because by the traditions of this ancient people, when a brother died without issue the next brother was expected not only to marry the widow but when a son was born, to recognize this son not as his but as the legal son of his deceased older brother; thus, the older son's line is carried on even though he has died without having a child. The second son of Judah, Onan, didn't like this arrangement, so he tried to circumvent it. He, too, died.

Now Judah might well have asked himself what was wrong with his sons, but being a rather average parent he concluded instead that something was wrong with his daughter-in-law, so therefore he didn't want to chance his third son with her. Then he did a quite dreadful thing as measured by their culture; he sent Tamar home to her family. Judah said this was a temporary measure until his son was old enough for marriage, but the community of those days didn't see it that way. They saw that Tamar was being rejected by her in-laws.

In time, Judah's wife died. The biblical writer tells us that "when Judah's time of mourning was over" he returned to his work. Tamar, meanwhile, realized that the third son was now grown, "yet she had not been given to him in marriage" (38:14). So she "put off her widow's garments" and wrapped herself instead in the concealing garb of a prostitute, her face so hidden that she could not be recognized, and stationed herself at a place where Judah would pass by. She knew the calendar; she knew that "Judah's time of mourning was over."

Sure enough, "he thought her to be a prostitute, for she had covered her face" (38:15). Judah had no payment with him, so he left behind "a pledge"—his signet, cord, and staff. But when Judah's associate brought payment to the supposed prostitute's tent, no one was to be found. Indeed, area residents said, "No prostitute has been here."

Three months later Judah learned that his daughter-in-law, Tamar, was pregnant "as a result of whoredom." Judah—apparently deciding now that Tamar was his responsibility—ordered that she be brought forward and burned for her crime. Tamar responded by sending him his signet, cord, and staff, explaining that it was the owner of these that had made her pregnant. Tamar's strategy was excellent; Judah replied, "She is more in the right than I, since I did not give her to my son Shelah" (38:26). She bore twins, Perez and Zerah.

Even if you don't like this story (and of course it's short on moral content), don't forget it, because it's here that (as the saying goes) the plot thickens. The author didn't interrupt the Joseph saga just to appeal to the baser tastes of his readers. Rather, he wanted them to know that while the plot was developing on one front in Joseph's sale into slavery, it was also developing on another front in a quite different way.

The two plot streams converge roughly two decades later. Through a series of misadventures in which Providence is quietly at work, Joseph has become the prime minister of Egypt. Because of his wise leadership, Egypt is the only country in a wide region with food; in fact, it has become the bread basket for a vast area. Among those who come to buy food are ten of Jacob's sons. Joseph recognizes them, but of course they don't recognize him. This man in his thirties, tonsured and adorned like an Egyptian and second in command in all of Egypt isn't likely to be confused with the seventeen-year-old they sold into slavery so long before.

I won't burden you with details here, even though they lend color to the story. Let me say only that when the brothers need to return to Egypt some months later for still more grain, their father bitterly resists the terms under which they must make their return. And it is Judah, fourth place or not, who with a growing sense of importance dares to be spokesperson in persuading his father.

When the brothers return to Egypt, Joseph—still unrecognized—puts them to a severe test. Under arrest, their lives in danger, how does the writer of Genesis identify them? *"Judah and his brothers* came to Joseph's house" (44:14, italics added). Not "the eleven brothers" nor "the sons of Jacob" but "Judah and his brothers." If this were a movie, the camera would slip quickly around the circle, then linger for a concerted study of Judah's face and form. Judah has become the center of the story, with the rest of the family serving as his supporting cast.

Some years later, with the whole family now in Egypt, father Jacob senses that death is near. He calls his sons together so he can tell them, like the good patriarch he is, "what will happen to you in days to come" (49:1). The longest statements are for Judah and Joseph. We aren't surprised that Jacob praises Joseph, because he's been his father's favorite all the way, but the signal words are spoken to Judah. He is "a lion's whelp." As such, "he crouches down, he stretches out like a lion." Thus the "scepter shall not depart from Judah, / nor the ruler's staff from between his feet, / until tribute comes to him" (49:9-10). That is, someday Judah's descendants are going to rule.

What follows is so extraordinary that I'm going to leave it for your own musing. Mind you, I'll give you my thinking; after all, that's part of the price of the book. Anyway, listen: speaking still of Judah and his future (including, of course, his descendants), Jacob says, "Binding his foal to the vine / and his donkey's colt to the choice vine, / he washes his garments in wine / and his robe in the blood of grapes" (49:11). In strange, rather exotic ways these lines make one think of a scene preparatory to Jesus' coming to Jerusalem, when he enters "on a colt, the foal of a donkey" (Matthew 21:5). As for garments washed in wine—what a strange instrument of cleansing! We might dye garments in wine, but *wash*? How strange!

The line that follows adds to the mystery. The robe shall be washed "in the blood of grapes." Naturally I read this from the context of my worship life as a Christian, as I think of the gathering in an upper room where Jesus poured wine for his disciples and after they had drunk it said to them, "This is my blood of the new covenant" (Mark 14:22-25). Blood of the grapes, indeed! This portion of my story is better understood by a poet than by a literalist. I'm not suggesting that you build a doctrine around it, but I urge you to let its beauty get beyond your intellectual mood to your affective side so you can warm your soul in it. And keep it in the back of your mind as our plot moves toward its completion. Whatever you think, just admit that the word Jacob spoke to his son Judah—this fourth son, this son with the very mixed history—was a strange word indeed.

Several generations slip by before Judah reappears in the story. It's at the conclusion of the little book of Ruth. We usually see this book as a beautiful love story, beginning with the loyalty of a daughter-in-law to her mother-in-law and ending with the marriage of a young widow, Ruth, to an older man, Boaz. At the wedding the older women of the community (Bethlehem) congratulate the mother-in-law, Naomi, on the family she will soon have through her daughter-in-law, ending with a very special wish: that her house may "be like the house of Perez, whom Tamar bore to Judah" (Ruth 4:12).

You remember the story of "Perez, whom Tamar bore to Judah," so you're likely to be surprised that anyone would want to keep the story alive, let alone make it the basis for a wedding toast. Obviously, something has happened in the time between Judah's relationship with Tamar and the book of Ruth. We learn what has happened as we come to the climax of this little book—the unlikely climax of a genealogy related to the son that is born to Ruth and Boaz.

Because we learn that not only is Boaz a descendant of Tamar and Judah, but that also he is the great-grandfather of David, Israel's most beloved king—and we sense that the significance of this little book of Ruth is not the story itself but that it is introducing us to Israel's greatest king, from the family of Judah. And of course we recall Jacob's word about Judah—that the scepter shall not depart from his line "nor the ruler's staff from between his feet" (Genesis 49:10).

For a devout Jew—or for that matter, for anyone interested in the story of Israel as a nation—the Judah detective story could rightly end here. For Christians, the story hasn't yet reached its climax.

Let's go to the opening chapter of the New Testament, which happens to be another genealogy—almost as if the writer wants to pick up where the book of Ruth left off. Matthew's genealogy wants to demonstrate that Jesus is "the son of David, the son of Abraham"—that is, that he has the ancestral qualifications to be God's Messiah. We've hardly begun before we read, "And Jacob the father of *Judah and his brothers* [remember that phrase!], and Judah the father of Perez and Zerah by Tamar, and Perez the father of Hezron" (Matthew 1:2-3, italics added).

So now we Christians see our crucial stake in Judah. It is from his line (tainted though it may seem) that Jesus of Nazareth, Savior of the World, is born. We remind ourselves also that we now know the people of Israel as *Jews*, a name derived from *Judah*, because in the course of time most of the tribes of Israel were lost by dispersion and intermarriage with conquering peoples; thus, the dominant people within Israel are the descendants of Judah.

And I should add an ironic note. The person who betrayed our Lord Jesus bore this same crucial name, Judah—or more specifically, *Judas*.

We're not quite done yet. The book of Revelation takes us into the presence of God, where at last the mysteries of the ages are to be consummated. When an angel introduces the one who is to open the scroll of mystery and judgment, he presents "the Lion of the tribe of Judah, the Root of David," the one who has conquered (Revelation 5:5). And of course you remember the words of Jacob, that Judah was to be "a lion's whelp," "like a lioness" (Genesis 49:9). No wonder, then, that when the twelve tribes of Israel are listed in Revelation 7:4-8, Judah is first in line.

It's quite a journey, from fourth place—a son born with no promise—to a descendant who stands before the throne of eternity as God's Son. I suspect that the beleaguered wife, Leah, said more than she knew when she rejoiced in that fourth son by naming him Judah: "This time I will praise the Lord!"

CHAPTER FIVE

WHO KILLED
MOTHER NATURE?

I've overstated the case. Mother Nature isn't dead yet, but it's not for lack of someone's trying. She's a lady tough to kill, partly because her life is of so many parts and partly because she has a quite unbelievable facility for turning potential demise into new destiny. Environmentalists tell us that elements of nature—what we call *species*—die every day. They not only estimate the number for today, they predict it for tomorrow or the next month. Sometimes you get the feeling that this decimation of species will continue until there's only one species left. But I'm getting ahead of myself.

Early in the human story, as the writer of Genesis tells it, a man named Cain killed his brother. He thought his crime was a secret, but God had observed it. "Where is your brother Abel?" God asked. Cain sidestepped the question like an expert witness in a courtroom trial, but God continued pursuit by producing an extraordinary witness. "Listen; your brother's blood is crying out to me from the ground" (Genesis 4:10). God then pronounced a sentence, and it came from this eyewitness, from the ground. "And now you are cursed from the ground, which has opened its mouth *to receive your brother's blood* from your hand. When you till the ground, it will no longer yield to you its strength" (4:11-12, italics added). This was fundamental bad news to Cain, since he was a tiller of the soil. Those pioneers who first broke the rocky soil of New England or the unrelenting dust of the northern prairies may sometimes have thought the soil was cursed for their sake, but to my knowledge God never said so.

But in God's notice to Cain, the Genesis historian showed that he was also a philosopher-theologian. He was telling us that a peculiar bond exists between humanity and the soil. The writer had said earlier that God had made the human creature out of the dust of the ground, so that the name by which we know him is a kind of pun: *Adam* from the Hebrew word for ground, *adamah.*

You get the point. We humans belong to the earth. It's more than poetry when a church leader or perhaps a friend says at the graveside, "Earth to earth . . . from the dust you have come and to the dust you shall return." Untended, the dead body becomes part of the soil in which it lies and from which the Genesis theologian-historian says that it came. So when Cain spilled his brother's blood (the very stuff of life) onto the ground, he was intruding on the relationship between humanity and the soil.

Now if I were preaching to you—a temptation I'll try to resist—I might raise a question about all those battlefields where we have distributed human bodies, or those places where bodies have emaciated in starvation. I would wonder how loud is the cry of blood from such soil. One of the major settings for blood, Auschwitz, has a monument with the inscription, "O earth, cover not their blood." Rowan Williams, Archbishop of Canterbury, says of that prayer, "There are things that should never, never be forgotten—Auschwitz is one of them."[1] If there is some peculiar tie between the soil of our planet and the blood of its dominant inhabitant, the human creature, then I venture that the earth will not cover the blood of Auschwitz or any other place where life is made cheap by the inhabitants of the planet. But I hadn't planned to preach just now. I'm just looking for a murderer.

I must say more, however, about the innate sacredness of the soil. Some very wise soul said it millennia ago, to prepare his countrymen for the land they were about to claim as their own. "You shall not pollute the land in which you live; for blood pollutes the land, and no expiation can be made for the land, for the blood that is shed in it, except by the blood of the one who shed it." Then the writer brings God into the issue. "You shall not defile the land in which you live, in which I also dwell; for I the LORD dwell among the Israelites" (Numbers 35:33-34).

You see the case that's developing here. The biblical writers began with the idea that God is the Creator—that's the way the whole epic starts in the book of Genesis. Therefore, God has a vested interest in all of this universe and apparently a unique interest in planet earth since, as far as we presently know, this is the only planet that sustains life—and particularly what we self-conscious humans refer to as "intelligent life." Furthermore, God has some standards as to how life should be lived on this planet, one of them being that we ought to take care of one another rather than destroying—thus the idea that when blood is shed the very earth itself is repulsed. We humans are not simply landholders, we are part of the essence of the earth. The soil is our kin. And, still more, the Lord God chooses to live in this land, so we ought to feel compelled to treat it and all of life with holy awe.

This planet has trouble with the misconduct of social and political bodies as well as with the sins of individual human beings. So when the fledgling nation of Israel moved toward their land of promise, the Lord advised them through Moses that they were getting this land because the current inhabitants had defiled it. "Thus the land became defiled; and I punished it for its iniquity, and the land vomited out its inhabitants" (Leviticus 18:25). Strong language. You might even call it repulsive. But before you draw back too delicately from this language, ponder the march of history. Is it possible that the violence of war and conquest is in some way related to nature's revulsion at the way we humans treat one another? And also the way we treat the rest of nature, including its intricate pattern of our planet's other inhabitants—animals, fish, and fowl—with disregard that is often quite criminal?

Let me call on some other detectives. Robert Royal reminds us of the "profound religious, political, economic, and even environmental turmoil" of the early fifteenth century, a time in which "something like 40 percent of the population disappeared," and "in some regions even more." Then he ponders: "As many modern environmentalists have devoutly wished, nature took its vengeance as human population decreased. Wolves multiplied and returned, even appearing in capital cities."[2]

Does Mother Nature, in fact, take vengeance on our human race because of our sins against her? And is it written into our very genetic code, part and parcel as we are of the soil? I offer another detective, Talking Hawk, a Native American from the Mohawk tribe. As he prepared for a sacred ceremony in which he would pray for the earth, he said, "Earth Mother is fighting back—not only from the four winds but also from underneath. Scientists call it global warming. We call it Earth Mother getting angry."[3] Is Talking Hawk's poetic language a more vigorous expression of the issue than the language of science? And is it, in fact, very much like the language of the Old Testament?

Speaking of poets, I bring another detective to the scene, perhaps an unlikely one, the nineteenth-century Jesuit priest/poet Gerard Manley Hopkins. As he put it, "The world is charged with the grandeur of God." He saw God's glory in "dappled things": a trout, a cow, and finches' wings. He didn't confuse nature with God, but he saw God's hand and thus God's beauty in the vast differentness of nature.

But with it all, Hopkins was filled with foreboding. He observed that generations of humans "have trod, have trod, have trod," until "all is seared with trade," and "wears man's smudge and shares man's smell." Hopkins expressed that fear in the latter decades of the nineteenth century, when we humans were still novices in our exploitation of Mother Earth. True, at that time the industrial revolution was gaining strength daily and the city skies in England, France, Germany, and the United States were already dark with progress, but even the most foresighted could not have imagined what would happen in the next one hundred years—especially as urbanization in Asia and South America makes the cities of Europe and America seem like sprawling villages.

But in his day, Hopkins had hope. I don't know how much of his hope was vested in us humans and our wisdom in dealing with our planet. If he could have known the reservoirs of human blood that would curse the soil in two World Wars of the twentieth century and the blood of Hitler's Holocaust and of Stalin's ruthless purgings, he might have been tempted to give up on the prospects for our planet. But I doubt it. I think he would still have written, "the Holy Ghost over the bent / World broods with warm breast and with ah! bright wings."[4] Because Hopkins believed that God has a stake in our creation. More likely than not he was familiar with the classical medieval proposition: "God and nature do nothing in vain." Certainly he possessed the conviction that God's purpose in our world must eventually triumph.

This was the profound conviction of the biblical writers, in the psalms and the words of prophets of the Old Testament and the books of Romans and Revelation in the New. Listen to Psalm 98:

> Let the sea roar, and all that fills it;
> the world and those who live in it.
> Let the floods clap their hands;
> let the hills sing together for joy
> at the presence of the LORD, for he is coming
> to judge the earth.
> He will judge the world with righteousness,
> and the peoples with equity. (98:7-9)

You get the point. The psalmist sees nature having a humongous party, including the sea and all its inhabitants as well as the world. The hills sing while the floods keep time by clapping their hands. Why? Because God has come to "judge the world with righteousness, / and the peoples with equity." The creation was made for harmony, and this harmony can express itself only when evil and inequity have been overcome.

The prophet Isaiah offers an equally idyllic scene:

> The wolf shall live with the lamb,
>   the leopard shall lie down with the kid,
> the calf and the lion and the fatling together,
>   and a little child shall lead them.
> The cow and the bear shall graze,
>   their young shall lie down together;
>   and the lion shall eat straw like the ox.
> The nursing child shall play over the hole of the asp,
>   and the weaned child shall put its hand on the adder's den.
> They will not hurt or destroy
>   on all my holy mountain;
> for the earth will be full of the knowledge of the LORD
>   as the waters cover the sea. (Isaiah 11:6-9)

The prophet sees a world where all the natural rapacity of the animal kingdom is gone. The wolf and the lamb, the calf and the lion—a relationship where ordinarily one is the diner and the other the lunch—now are companions. How can this be? Isaiah answers when he tells us that "the lion shall eat straw like the ox." The way of life is so beatific that a child can lead these beasts—can, in fact, play on the hole of the venomous snake.

But note again the secret of this new quality in nature. It is the result of a new kind of political and social order where the ruler (God's Messiah, as the church has interpreted the passage since its earliest days) will "judge the poor" with righteousness, and will "decide with equity for the meek of the earth" (11:4). This is quite different from the world of politics as most of our planet knows it. Even in America, where we pride ourselves on justice and equality, it is still too often the case that you're better off if "you know the right people," and where quite too often the well-to-do suburban teenager gets a different kind of justice than a ghetto dweller of the same age. And note too that this is no saccharine, namby-pamby system: this ruler will "strike the earth with the rod of his mouth, / and with the breath of his lips / he shall kill the wicked" (11:4).

But back to our detective story: it is in this setting of human justice that we have the picture of nature sublimely at peace.

The crucial investigator in this case of "Who Killed Mother Nature?" is the Apostle Paul. His argument is tucked into a deep theological discussion of sin and salvation in the Epistle to the Romans: "The whole creation is on tiptoe to see the wonderful sight of the sons of God coming into their own" (Romans 8:19 J. B. Phillips). Because at present the creation is "subjected to futility"; it is in "bondage to decay" (8:20-21). This bondage is so severe that "the whole creation has been groaning in labor pains until now." And we human beings are suffering with nature: "not only the creation, but we ourselves, who have the first fruits of the Spirit, groan inwardly while we wait for adoption, the redemption of our bodies" (8:22-23).

So as that remarkable Episcopal clergywoman Fleming Rutledge puts it, "To be the church means to be a community of solidarity with the whole creation, waiting with hope for the glorious redemption that God brings."[5]

Here, then, is the case in what is happening to Mother Nature. Murder is in process, and it has been for a very long time. And the perpetrators are the caretakers, human beings. As the book of Genesis says, God gave us human beings dominion over the earth and trusted us to take good care of it. God took an audit when the earth was placed in our care and recorded that "indeed, it was very good" (Genesis 1:31). It's quite clear that it isn't that good today and that, despite some earnest efforts by an increasing variety of people, the situation is still getting worse.

Professional environmentalists are doing an admirable job at the nuts-and-bolts level of the problem. They report the decimation of species (God's creation, as believers see it), and the astonishing trashing of our planet—its water, its air, its soil. They've come up with a motto that Christians ought to be more ready than anyone to adopt: *live simply so that others can simply live.* We can't go on treating this planet as if we were on an eternal drunken spending spree.

The Scriptures take us a step further. They tell us that we human beings have a mystical tie to this planet. It isn't simply the place where we live and the source of our food and water and air. It's more than that: we belong to each other. We are ourselves dust, and when we mistreat the planet we are cutting ourselves off from our own essential being. Ever since Cain, every time we spill the blood of another person, the ground cries out against us. As I see it, this cry is just as distinct whether it be murder, war, the starvation that comes from our exploitation of others or our neglect of their needs.

And of course our problem is deeply spiritual, because our destructive conduct comes from greed, selfishness, indifference to others, thoughtless living. These are spiritual problems, and they call for transforming redemption. What's more, we are—every day—part either of the problem or of the solution. The Bible is confident that Mother Nature will not be destroyed. But we decide whether we will be among the planet's murderers or among its saviors.

In Dostoyevsky's *Crime and Punishment,* when Sonya leads Rodya to redemption she pleads with him to "kiss the earth, because you have sinned before it as well." He does so, and "there, in that filthy earth, he was filled with delight and happiness."[6] He had made peace with the soil to which we all belong: from which we came and to which we shall return. It is a planet that was made for godly living, and when we treat it otherwise we are out of sync with the universe and with our own souls.

CHAPTER SIX

MAKING DO WITH REMNANTS

I should tell you right off that I have mixed feelings about this story. The psychological type would say that my feelings are *conflicted*. I wouldn't go that far, but perhaps that shows I'm not the psychological type.

Still, when I give you the background you may develop a whole theory about my personality. Here it is. My mother was a seamstress—a woman who found pride in making clothes, whether for pay or for fun, for women or girls or babies. In my growing-up years, during the Great Depression, she made my shirts, which was for me at times a matter of some discomfort. Since I was by this time the only child left at home, Mother took me on her shopping trips to be the bag carrier. This was a humiliating assignment for an eleven- or twelve-year-old boy, but especially so when she made what was for her the most important point of any shopping trip, a visit to the remnant counter.

Every department store had one in those days. They were visited solely by women—passionately intent, highly competitive women—all of them looking for a piece of cloth that could be made into some project and that held promise of being a bargain. Remnants were the leftovers from the bolts of cloth, and they were so big an element of business in a day when almost every woman was a bit of a seamstress or knew someone who was. Depending on the nature of the cloth, the remnants were anything from a scrap of six or eight inches and the width of the bolt to perhaps a yard and a half or two yards. But the people who shopped for bargains were connoisseurs. They could look at a bedraggled scrap and see a skirt, a scarf, a child's dress, or a quilt patch or two.

This is where I got my mixed feelings. It was depressing, at my age at the time, to stand on one leg, then the other, wishing I had four more legs on which to spend time, while all these experts—sometimes merciless competitors—sorted through the shapeless pile, all the time talking professionally about what might be done with a given piece. You learned in time that when a woman said, "That piece would look lovely on a two-year-old," it meant really, "This is a remnant I'm not interested in." But even while I hated standing and waiting, I was somehow fascinated that these women could see so much promise in such a confusion of leftovers.

Then one day I discovered that God had a penchant for remnants. It came to me early in my Bible reading: because *remnant* was a word I knew so well, when I came upon it in the Bible I wondered how it got there. I took the word in stride when it referred to a remnant of a garment or of meat or oil, but when I got to the Old Testament prophets the word began to be all about *people*. That's when I began to feel that God liked the word, almost as if the divine had more interest in remnants than in the full bolt, so to speak.

The first remnant in our story isn't identified as such, but there's no mistaking him. A bargain sale had been going on for a generation or more, a situation in which human beings—these wonderful creatures, so full of potential, made in the image of God—had become so distorted that "every imagination of the thoughts of their hearts was only evil continually" (Genesis 6:5). We humans are constantly offered some deal for which we pay our time, our money, our glands, and—eventually—our souls; and we decide how much we think we're worth. The ancient generation at this point in the biblical story was selling itself cheap, and it looked as if the whole bolt of cloth was gone; after all, the writer said that "*all* flesh had corrupted its ways upon the earth" (6:12, italics added). It sounds as if the whole corpus had been sold out.

But there was a remnant, a man named Noah. He was "a righteous man, blameless in his generation," and he walked with God (6:9). He was all that was left—he and his three sons and their wives. God took delight in this remnant and through them saved the human race. This is a special fact about the divine remnant business, that God—like any good seamstress—finds special use for remnants: no matter how ordinary the remnant may look or how unpromising, they're the hope of the future. Always. Mind you, I believe in democracy and majority votes and all that sort of thing, but always pay attention to the minority because the odds are good that they will set life's sail for tomorrow.

What I've just said lets you know that this is a different sort of detective story. Usually we're looking for a villain, a perpetrator of evil. But in this matter of remnants the key figure wears the white hat. Well, sometimes at first glance you'll think it's a dunce's cap rather than a hero's hat, because the remnant type is almost always a contrarian, voting against the odds. An unknown New Testament writer tells us in the book of Hebrews that you can recognize these people because they have *faith*. These are people, he says, who are assured about "things hoped for," and who have "conviction about things not seen" (Hebrews 11:1), and if that outlook doesn't mark you for condescending smiles, nothing will.

If I had time, I'd tell you about more of these particular personalities—like Abraham, Sarah, Moses, Rahab—every one of them working against the odds so often that much of the time they were objects of scorn. A good many of them died for what they believed, and the one who tells their story says they were people "of whom the world was not worthy" (Hebrews 11:38), which is pretty strong praise. But they were the remnant type, still doing their thing long after the culture of their times had sold out.

And if it's not bad enough to be a leftover on life's bargain counter, the writer of Hebrews adds a further unnerving element. After telling the stories of all those remnant types the writer continues, "Yet all these, though they were commended for their faith, did not receive what was promised, since God had provided something better so that they would not, apart from us, be made perfect" (Hebrews 11:39-40). This is the final indignity: the remnant often doesn't get to see the purpose for which it was chosen. But more of that later.

I want to call in two witnesses. They are specialists in remnanting, because they were prophets. That is, they had a special gift for looking at life and history, and seeing meaning that everyone else missed. That's the remnant mentality. It's the thing I saw in my mother and all those other women who hovered over the remnant counter. They could look at throwaway stuff and see in it some beautiful prospect. If I may use a theological term, when they looked at remnants they set off on a process of redemption. Well, redemption was the bread-and-butter business of the prophets.

The Hebrew prophets were good at this sort of thing because they did most of their work on their nation's night shift. There never seemed to be much market for prophets when things were going well. They were called in when some enemy nation was arming against them or when moral decadence was at such an abysmal point that it couldn't go any lower. They had the instincts of a moral detective: they could look at a situation and see where it was leading. They would then issue a warning, but of course this kind of assignment didn't make them popular.

Isaiah—he of the golden voice—got such an assignment early in his prophetic career. When he was still basking in the wonder of the divine vision of his call, the Lord said, "Go then, said he, and give a message to this people of mine." What kind of vision? "Though a tenth of their number remain, it is but empty show, like leafage of terebinth or oak that needs pruning; only a remnant of it will be left, the true stock of holiness" (Isaiah 6:13).[1] I can't imagine telling a nation that only a tenth of them will be left, and that even that tenth will be "an empty show," but Isaiah was commissioned to deliver such a message.

His nation, Israel, had believed from the days when they escaped Egyptian slavery under the leadership of Moses that they had a unique mission under God. In a peculiar way they were to be the head of the nations of the earth. Not in military power or in land size, but in moral authority, the kind of authority that would make other nations turn to them for ethical leadership. Of course, they were human enough that they often projected this role of holy leadership into all the other elements of power that nations and individuals ordinarily seek. They had a brief period, under the reigns of King David and King Solomon, when they were a significant force in the politics of the ancient Middle East, which made them dream of continuing, growing power. And as I just said, it's natural to dream of the kind of power that this world tends to cherish, but it's very difficult to be content with something as ephemeral as moral and ethical influence. You can't quantify such influence the way you can measure armies, munitions, and industrial wealth.

So Israel kept hoping they would become a power to be reckoned with. Instead the prophet Isaiah—who tended to be a much more positive sort, unlike Jeremiah or Amos, for instance—announced that they might be diminished to a tenth of their present strength, and that even that tenth would be hardly more than a stump. Not to worry: only a *remnant* will be left, but it will be *quality*. It will be "the true stock of holiness." And since holiness— that is, moral and ethical character—was God's purpose in calling out this nation, this would mean that they were a true success.

This remnant theme was so dominant in Isaiah's mind that he named his son Shearjashub. There's probably a footnote in your Bible to tell you that the boy's name meant "a remnant shall return" (Isaiah 7:3). Every time Isaiah looked at his son, he was reminded of God's plan for his nation: they might go through desert places, where the future was palpably bleak, and they might seem to teeter on the edge of nonexistence, but God would accomplish the divine purpose with a remnant. In God's hand, a remnant is enough.

This was the mood that kept Isaiah and his kind believing in the future. "The surviving remnant of the house of Judah," he wrote, "shall again take root downward, and bear fruit upward; for from Jerusalem a remnant shall go out, and from Mount Zion a band of survivors. The zeal of the LORD of hosts will do this" (Isaiah 37:31-32). I think Isaiah meant that the Lord's zeal for his people, Israel (Judah), and for the righteousness they were meant to represent was the guarantee that a remnant was sufficient to bring victory. But sometimes, as I've said, I have a feeling that God is simply prejudiced in favor of remnants.

Still, being a remnant is no guarantee of success. The issue is the quality and the potential of the remnant. In the prophet Jeremiah's time a delegation of people, led by the commanders of the army, came to the prophet to appeal their case as "this remnant. For there are only a few of us left out of many" (Jeremiah 42:2). Jeremiah told them what they ought to do ("O remnant of Judah, thus says the LORD of hosts" [42:15]). But when the delegation went counter to Jeremiah's counsel, they were told that their "remnant" that was so determined to go its own way, would "perish" (44:12). The issue is the quality and purpose of the remnant, not its size. "Look, Lord, I'm small so, of course, you're on my side"—to which God replies, "Small isn't the issue. Are you good small or bad small? I'm looking for a holy remnant."

Jesus came preaching about a Kingdom—the Kingdom of God, the Kingdom of heaven. This is heady stuff, and it's no wonder that people hailed him as the one for whom their nation had been waiting and that even his closest companions, the disciples, anticipated positions in his empire. But Jesus coded the remnant philosophy into so much of his teaching about his kingdom. The Kingdom of God, he said, is like a farmer who sows seed broadcast, and most of it (three-quarters, it appears) produces nothing, but a small portion (a remnant?) is wonderfully effective. His Kingdom is like a grain of mustard seed, tiny and insignificant, but it becomes a tree. His Kingdom is like yeast in a homemaker's hand: it's like nothing, yet it controls three measures of flour (see Matthew 13). This is remnant talk—leftovers, things easily overlooked or discarded. But Jesus said that this is the stuff with which the Kingdom of God is built.

Jesus made his point by the team he assembled. Two people of demonstrated potential, Nicodemus and Joseph of Arimathea, honored Jesus at his burial, but they never joined the public team, and we hear no more of them after Easter. The team was made up, basically, of two parts: the twelve disciples and a little group of women from Galilee who often provided for the needs of Jesus and the disciples. It's hard for us today to realize it, but there wasn't a game-breaker in the crowd. Not, that is, until they had spent time with Jesus. They were very much the remnant type—some fishermen, a tax collector, a small-time revolutionary, village women following a village carpenter.

Yet, when the story comes to a climax, it's a scene where "a great multitude that no one could count, from every nation, from all tribes and peoples and languages" stand before the throne to declare their loyalty. How do you get from remnants—Israel, Judah, and the church; Noah, Abraham, martyrs, and prophets—to a multitude no one can number? How does this happen?

Is it that God prefers remnants? Paul, who was a better-than-average detective, suggested as much. He said, "God chose what is low and despised in the world, things that are not, to reduce to nothing things that are, so that no one might boast in the presence of God" (1 Corinthians 1:28-29).

But perhaps there's something more that Paul doesn't get into at this point. Perhaps it's that God sees potential where common wisdom does not. Anyone can predict that the fleet of foot will win the race. Extraordinary vision (imagination?) is required to expect an uncoordinated stumble-foot to do so. As I said earlier, I admired the creativity of those women who were gathered with my mother at the remnant counter; they could see possibilities in fragments. I see this as a divine gift.

Perhaps too God works with remnants because majorities have a way of deteriorating. Majorities easily become mobs, on the one hand, or complacent dullards on the other. Drunk with the power of their numbers, a majority can ride roughshod on the rights of others; or comfortable in their strength, they can become dull to the voice of God and the challenge of changing times. That's why you do well to listen to minority voices—in politics, in philosophy, in science, wherever—because often they've caught an insight that the poll-reading majority have missed.

It may be that you'd like to raise another question with me. Will heaven be a remnant, a very small crowd: "Me and my wife, my son David and his wife, we four and no more"? Well, as I read the Scriptures, God is going to win big. The role of the remnant is not simply to survive but to reach, influence, and bring to potential the faltering rest. And God works with a remnant because it's better to have a few who have a purpose than a multitude who function uncertainly.

That brings it back to you and me. If we're one of God's people, does it mean that God found us on a remnant counter? Quite possibly. Indeed, from a theological point of view, I suspect that it's almost a certainty. If you don't like that classification, you're cutting yourself off from a pretty noble company, from people like Noah, Abraham,

Sarah, David, Isaiah, Jeremiah, Paul, the women of Galilee, and the apostles.

Being a remnant is a precarious calling, and a humbling one, because you have to be willing to be used the way the Purchaser desires. But it's also very exciting because you never know how beautiful you may someday become. In truth, you may not know until eternity.

CHAPTER SEVEN

CHRISTMAS WOMEN

Women have a special claim on Christmas. We men play our part, but at best it tends to be a supporting role and at worst it's a getting-in-the-way, ruining-everything experience. Men can choose a Christmas tree (sometimes), set it in its base, and fasten the top ornament, but women put on the final touches that give a tree its ultimate elegance. Men want desperately to find the right present but discover that "desperately" is not enough; one needs a certain instinct that comes in limited supply in the male gene. Men frequently eat Christmas cookies but rarely do they bake them.

The role of women and Christmas is in truth a very long story. For centuries artists have made the point without even trying. No one can estimate how many paintings and sculptures have portrayed the Mother and Child, but only rarely does Joseph appear. There's a theological reason, of course, because in the biblical story Joseph is the surrogate father: Jesus is the Son of God, born to the Virgin Mary. But that doesn't diminish the point concerning women and Christmas; it only empowers it.

As I said a moment ago, it's a long story. How long? Well, try going back to the book of Genesis in the Bible. That is, try going back to the Garden of Eden—or more precisely, to someplace just outside the Garden, some place east of Eden.

Adam and Eve ruined their Garden spot. Some lay the blame heavily on Eve, but it's clear that Adam didn't exercise much masculine restraint when Eve began doing business with the persuasive serpent. As they were expelled from Eden, God gave both judgment and promise to Eve. The judgment had to do with "pangs in childbearing" and in the nature of her relationship to her husband. The promise came in a roundabout way, in the curse that was placed on the serpent:

> "I will put enmity between you and the woman,
>   and between your offspring and hers;
> he will strike your head,
>   and you will strike his heel." (Genesis 3:15)

The curse on the serpent was for the woman a promise of revenge: her offspring (or her *seed*, as many translations put it) will crush the head of the one who got her in trouble and who took paradise from her and her husband and their descendants.

Eve took the promise seriously—so seriously that when she brought forth her first child, a son, she named him *Cain:* "I have got me a man with the LORD."[1] Eve saw herself in partnership with God in the birth of this first child and in anticipation of what this child would do in righting the wrong she had suffered. When the second son, Abel, was born, his name received no such defining significance. Clearly for Eve he didn't carry the hope of deliverance or the burden of responsibility.

But Cain didn't turn out the way Eve expected. Of the two sons, Abel was the one who by his faith pleased God. Cain, instead of bruising the serpent's head, seemed rather to have been infected with the serpent's venom and became the first murderer, making murder a family affair as he killed his younger brother.

Well, that doesn't seem like a very good start for women in the Christmas story, but I have to tell you the story the way it is, not the way you and I want it to be. Besides, as all of us know, many a later Christmas story has been tainted with its share of pain—sometimes loneliness, sometimes selfishness, sometimes greed, and often just a lot of simple misunderstanding. But now I'm beginning to sermonize, and that's not what this story is all about.

In order to continue the story I have to make a long leap to the book of Matthew in the New Testament. Actually, the next event is originally reported in the book of Genesis, only a few pages and several generations after Eve's disappointment with Cain, but we don't get the importance of it when we're reading Genesis so I'll make the Matthew move. If I were to tell you the next step by way of Genesis I could build more suspense, but the suspense might be so well-hidden that you'd fall asleep on me—and I can't have that happen.

Matthew begins the Christmas story in the most prosaic of ways. Eventually he gets to Joseph and Mary and the wise men, but he begins as if perhaps he had a legal brief in mind: "An account of the genealogy of Jesus the Messiah, the son of David, the son of Abraham" (Matthew 1:1). This is a strategic beginning because Matthew wants his readers to know that Jesus has the right family line. The excitement follows, but you won't catch it unless you're a pretty fair Bible student or unless you've read an earlier chapter in this book.

It's also the first time a woman is mentioned in the Christmas story in the New Testament: "and Judah the father of Perez and Zerah by Tamar" (Matthew 1:3). A twenty-first century person may feel that the woman is slipping in through the back door, perhaps resenting that the language is all too conventional: *by Tamar,* as though a woman is worth no more than her ability to be the carrier of life from one generation to another.

But on second thought, there's surely nothing ignominious about being the transmitter of life. Without such a role, the human race would simply cease to exist. Adam seemed to recognize as much when in a moment of devastatingly crucial insight he named his wife *Eve,* which means mother of *life.* So let us not be condescending about that simple line *by Tamar.* That's how it happens that we're all here, because someone was the channel of life through the perilous journey of the ages.

Matthew is directing our attention back to the infamous story in Genesis 38 in which Judah, one of the twelve sons of Israel and the progenitor of the most significant tribe, first treats his daughter-in-law disrespectfully (and illegally, by the standards of the ancient world), then impregnates her, not knowing it is his daughter-in-law, leading to the birth of twins. And the elder of these twins, Perez became part of the family line leading to David, Israel's most beloved king, and eventually to Jesus, known to billions for more than twenty centuries as the Savior of the world.

But the woman, Tamar, is the novelist's essence of a damaged product. She was widowed twice in erratic ways while still probably in her teens (folks married young in that world), then shamefully pushed aside by her father-in-law. But not one to be put down, Tamar found a way to defeat her father-in-law at his own game, and in the process she became mother to his sons. It isn't a pretty story, but it reminds us again that the Bible doesn't seek to be a pretty book but a *true* book; and life, as most of us know, sometimes isn't pretty. The secret, of course, is in the beauty (which is a much bigger word than *pretty*) that can be brought out of the ugliness of life. So it is that out of Tamar's precipitous story we have an ancestor for King David and ultimately for Jesus of Nazareth.

But if you're looking for relief after Tamar's story, you won't get it in the next personality. Her name was Rahab and she too slips into the story with a brief byline: "and Salmon the father of Boaz by Rahab" (Matthew 1:5). Rahab's story appears in the book of Joshua. When the nomadic nation of Israel set out to invade the land that was to become their home, their first stop was Jericho, a storied, walled-in city. Joshua sent two men to spy out the territory, and they "entered the house of a prostitute whose name was Rahab, and spent the night there" (Joshua 2:1). The king of Jericho learned that spies were in his city and that they might be in the house of Rahab. Rahab chose to protect the spies—surely at the peril of her own life—and she did so as an act of faith. "I know that the Lord has given you the land," she told the spies. Then she made her appeal: "Now then, since I have dealt kindly with you, swear to me by the LORD that you in turn will deal kindly with my family" (Joshua 2:12).

The spies kept their word, and when the army of Israel marched triumphantly into the city, Joshua instructed the two spies, "Go into the prostitute's house, and bring the woman out of it and all who belong to her, as you swore to her" (Joshua 6:22). They did so, and as the sacred historian concludes this segment of the story, he adds this comment from his vantage point several generations later: "Her family has lived in Israel ever since" (Joshua 6:25).

So what shall we say about Rahab? Well, first of all we note that the Bible records her name. Some people remain anonymous in the Bible. As a matter of fact, such is the case with the two men who spied out the land. They are referred to a number of times but always simply as "the two men" or "the men." I find it fascinating that these spies—heroic, derring-do figures who must surely have been heralded through their nation for leading the way in this spectacular military achievement—are anonymous, while the woman in whose house (or shall we say, whose *establishment*) they stayed is identified by name repeatedly.

And we know this about her too, that she was a prostitute. The biblical historian says so at least three times. He adds no adjective to justify or condemn her, just matter-of-factly identifies her: this is what she was.

But somehow, also, she was a *believer*. Living among a pagan people, making her living by an immoral practice, she somehow had a sensitivity to God that compelled her to put her life in danger in order to protect the Israelite spies. And in case you think it was just a case of her street smarts, remember how she spoke of the matter to the spies: "I know that the LORD has given you the land. . . . For we have heard how the LORD dried up the waters of the Red Sea before you. . . . The LORD your God is indeed God in heaven above and on earth below" (Joshua 2:9-11).

Rahab's sensitivity to God is, in fact, so significant that two New Testament writers praise her: James for her works and the book of Hebrews for her faith (James 2:25, Hebrews 11:31). How is it that this woman—with no access to conventional sacred writings, living what society would call a marginal life—was a woman of such remarkable spiritual gifts? I can't answer my question in a brief logical explanation, but I can say that I have read variations on her story scores of times in Christian literature, and I have known untold numbers of persons whose spiritual heritage is equally difficult to analyze.

At any rate, Rahab is the third woman in our Christmas story.

And then there's Ruth. Boaz became "the father of Obed *by Ruth*" (Matthew 1:5, italics added). Ruth backed into the Christmas story. Hundreds of years before the first Christmas, an Israelite family from Bethlehem migrated to the country of Moab because of a famine in their own land. Eventually the two sons in the family married Moabite girls, even though there was a long-standing prohibition against association between Israel and Moab. Misfortune settled in on this family so that in a relatively short period the father and the two sons all died, leaving three widows: the mother-in-law, Naomi, and her two young daughters-in-law, Ruth and Orpah. Naomi knew that her only chance of survival was to return to Bethlehem where there was some family property and where she had some distant kin who might care for her. Ruth insisted on going with her:

Where you go, I will go;
  where you lodge, I will lodge;
your people shall be my people,
  and your God my God. (Ruth 1:16)

So Ruth stayed with her mother-in-law, Naomi, when Naomi returned to Bethlehem and, in a quite lovely May and September romance, married a relative of Naomi's (and thus a relative of Ruth's deceased husband). From their union came the child Obed, who would be an ancestor of King David and eventually—as the New Testament book of Matthew notes—an ancestor of Jesus, the Babe of Bethlehem.

From our sentimental vantage point Ruth looks like just the kind of person one would want somewhere in the family tree. What more could one ask than a daughter-in-law who would pledge to stand by her mother-in-law through every circumstance, even to the point of vowing, "Where you die, I will die— / there will I be buried" (Ruth 1:17)? But her story isn't quite that simple. As a Moabite she was under something of an ancient curse. When the fledgling nation of Israel was making its interminable journey from Egypt to Canaan, the Moabites and the Ammonites refused them any hospitality on their journey. So Israel vowed that no Ammonite or Moabite would be "admitted to the assembly of the LORD" (Deuteronomy 23:3)—even to the tenth generation, which was a rather roundabout way of saying, "Not at all."

In the language of prejudice Ruth was a *foreigner*, a word that can be spoken with an accent that means *outsider*. Instead, by grace and providence, Ruth became the ancestress of Israel's most heralded king and herself one of the nation's most beloved women. Now we find her in the Christmas story. She bore the burden of no sin or crime of her own, only an ancient ethnic prejudice—the kind of burden that throughout history has destroyed millions. And Ruth is one of our Christmas women.

And then there was Bathsheba. I won't go into her story in detail. You probably know it in some fashion or other.

Bathsheba was the wife of a military hero, Uriah. One day while Uriah was away at war, King David saw—from the vantage point of his palace height—the beautiful Bathsheba bathing on her rooftop. Smitten by her beauty, he brought her to the palace; committed adultery with her; and eventually, to cover their relationship and Bathsheba's ensuing pregnancy, arranged for Uriah's death. The son of that union died in infancy, but David and Bathsheba's next son was Solomon, who succeeded to the throne of Israel and thus becomes part of the Christmas story as an ancestor of Jesus.

Matthew's Gospel puts it quite directly: "And David was the father of Solomon *by the wife of Uriah*" (Matthew 1:6; italics added). Matthew seems not only to be unembarrassed by the story but to make a point of it, identifying Bathsheba not by name but by her former relationship; indeed—not even offering the kindness of saying *"formerly* the wife of Uriah."* Matthew couldn't have handled it more effectively if he were the town gossip.

Then, finally, the line of Christmas women comes to its climax in Mary, the young girl from Nazareth. Both Matthew and Luke, the two books that tell the Christmas story, make clear that she was a virgin (Matthew 1:18-25; Luke 1:26-35). Luke emphasizes the quality of Mary's character: she is "favored" of God, and when she is called to her unique assignment she responds in the fashion not of the teenager she was but of a mature saint: "Here am I, the servant of the Lord: let it be with me according to your word" (Luke 1:38).

So that's how we see Mary. When we speak her name it is often with a defining noun: the *Virgin* Mary. Beyond doubt, this peasant girl from an obscure village is the most revered woman in the history of our human race—so revered, in fact, that we have a word to describe excessive adoration: *Mariolatry.*

But with all of that we are compelled at some point to ponder the question Mary raised with the angel when she was told that she would "conceive in (her) womb and bear a son," and that he would "be called the Son of the Most High" (Luke 1:31-32): *"How can this be, since I am a virgin?"* (Luke 1:34, italics added). One doesn't need much imagination to realize the askance with which people in Mary's village looked at this girl who was pregnant before marriage. For the devout for twenty-one centuries later, it is a story bathed in the soft light of reverence and sentiment. For the people of first-century Nazareth it was a story to be whispered by women at the village well.

So, as I said a while ago, women have a special claim on Christmas. It has been true since Eve looked forward with mistaken expectation to her first son, through a series of rather marginal stories. You can think of it what you will. As I read it, I see a God who isn't put off by sinners, who has no ethnic prejudices, and who is never defeated by our human errors. A God who writes a great mystery story— even and especially at Christmastime.

Think of it the next time you sit in a Christmas Eve service at your church or in a social gathering in someone's living room and you sing, "round yon Virgin Mother and Child." Think of it, and as you whisper the line once more to your soul, give thanks to God.

CHAPTER EIGHT

JOSEPH THE DREAMER

It may just be a coincidence. If that's all it is I won't apologize too profusely for leading you down this road, because at the very least coincidences are fun. And now and then—just often enough to pique our fancy and to keep us believing that maybe there's something more to coincidence than mere coincidence—coincidences make us shake our heads and wonder if there's more present than meets the eye.

My dictionary defines *coincidence* as "a striking occurrence of two or more events at one time apparently by mere chance."[1] This definition pretty well disqualifies my story from being coincidence because the two events were not "at one time" and in truth they may not even be "striking." Still, when you're on the detective beat you don't like to rule out things just because tough reason is against you. Who can guess how many mysteries would never have been solved if some struggling gumshoe hadn't bet his coat on a "mere coincidence"?

Yet, having said all of that, I'll confess that my coincidence isn't a really big deal. But a coincidence doesn't have to be earth-shaking in order to be intriguing. You simply take it for what it's worth. In this instance, it seems to me to be an interesting story, and if you'll let me, I'll tell it.

A great many years ago (two millennia ago, in fact), a Jewish family had a son. He was born into a good, working-class family. They weren't well-known people, though they did come from good stock. As a matter of fact, if you went back some twenty-five generations or more on their family tree, they could claim King David as an ancestor. As a result, they had reason to claim proudly that Bethlehem was their ancestral home because that was also the hometown for King David. By this time, of course, there were hundreds, indeed thousands, of people who referred to David as their ancestor. After all, David had had a large number of sons and daughters, so after a period of so many generations a great many people could name him as their ancestor.

But as I've already indicated, the family I'm talking about no longer had any social status to make them feel like kings. They were working folk, very possibly salt-of-the-earth kinds of people, but not especially different from the other people in their village.

In time they had a son, and they named him *Joseph*. It was a good name to give a boy, a kind of vote of confidence in his future. The name went back into the ancestry of their people all the way to one of the original twelve sons of Jacob, the patriarch from whom the tribes of Israel came. In most ways this earlier Joseph had been the most admirable of the twelve boys, though he had a period when one worried as to how he would grow up, spoiled as he was by his father. But he had been special, no doubt about it. Some of Israel's sons, like Issachar and Zebulun, seem in retrospect to have been nonentities, and others like Reuben and Levi embarrassed themselves and their family. But Joseph had been a noble, heroic figure. So, many years later, when this family with ties to Bethlehem decided to name their son Joseph, it was a proud act on their part and perhaps even a presumptuous one. They belonged to a culture that took names seriously, so giving a son such a strategic name was no casual matter.

After all, the first Joseph had eventually become the prime minister of the great empire of Egypt, and as such had developed a program of statesmanship that in some ways could serve as a model for centuries to come. In the process Joseph saved not only the lives of most of the common people of Egypt but also the lives of thousands of people from surrounding countries who had also been caught in the great, extended famine. Eventually Joseph was able to save the lives of his own family—his father, his siblings, and their children. So when a Jewish family, many centuries later, had a son and called him Joseph, they were thinking big—not necessarily in the sense of their son becoming a major political figure but perhaps in hoping that he would have something of the nobility of character that marked the first recorded holder of that name.

(You know, some contemporary sports fans—hard-core fans, that is—name a son or a daughter after some very successful athlete, some golfer or racetrack driver or home run hitter or multimillion-dollar quarterback, hoping their son or daughter will pick up some of the aura from that athlete and become equally famous someday. Other people do the same thing with entertainers. And of course some do this with political leaders, and once in a very great while with a scholar or a religious leader. They're thinking big! They hope that by giving their child a special name their child will become a special person, perhaps famous in his or her own right.)

So the parents of this baby boy were thinking big when they named him Joseph. They felt they had something special—or they were praying that he would become very special. And they named him Joseph.

By our judgment, Joseph's life was altogether ordinary, a village boy in a village where most of the time nothing special happened. He learned the carpenter's trade, perhaps from his father or perhaps from some other village builder. Apparently he had the gifts and skills and ambition to become a good carpenter, and he worked at it.

Then the boy, while still in his teens, fell in love with a village girl, a girl named Mary. Many girls were named Mary in those days, but as far as young Joseph was concerned, there was only one Mary. Their families were sympathetic to their friendship, and they agreed to the rather intricate system of courtship. First there was engagement. This could be arranged by the parents, perhaps even when the boy and girl were still children, or it could come later. The second stage came when the boy and girl were probably in what we would call their mid-teens. This stage was betrothal, and it lasted a full year. During this year the couple was seen as husband and wife, except that they couldn't engage in physical union. But the betrothal was of such significance that to break it was not simply what modern law might call "breach of promise," it was so serious that it could be broken only by a divorce. And if by chance the man died in the betrothal period, the woman was known as "a virgin who is a widow." At the end of the year of betrothal the couple was officially and fully married. I tell you all of this because it will help you understand this young man named Joseph— especially so you'll have some feeling for Joseph at what happened next. Sometime during the year of betrothal he got shocking news. The Bible puts the matter clearly, even if rather delicately. When "Mary had been engaged to Joseph, but before they lived together, she was found to be with child from the Holy Spirit" (Matthew 1:18).

The biblical writer doesn't tell us how Joseph got this shattering news. It's my feeling that Mary herself told him. I don't know how she could have kept such news entirely to herself and particularly how she could have kept it from Joseph. Nevertheless, she needed more than human courage to speak the word, and when she delivered it she got the worst possible response.

Well, I take that back. The worst response would have been the response the law of the times made possible for Joseph. It was his right to disown her completely and to make her a public spectacle. But because Joseph was, the historian tells us, "a righteous man," and because he didn't want to expose Mary to public disgrace, he "planned to dismiss her quietly." He was understandably bewildered.

He loved this village girl, a girl he had watched grow up. He had dreamed about marrying her. Now, however, he could only conclude that she had betrayed him. He couldn't find a reason for such betrayal, couldn't see anything in her previous conduct to hint of its happening, but there was no escaping the fact. A quiet divorce was his only recourse.

But that's when Joseph began dreaming. Mind you, he may have dreamed a good deal prior to this time. I'm sure he had his wide-awake dreams; a man waiting to marry does a good deal of that kind of dreaming. And of course he did his share of the kind of dreaming all of us do, the kind where we can hardly reconstruct the dream the next morning and to which we attach no significance. But I don't know if he had ever dreamed in the grand biblical sense, the kind of thing Elihu had in mind when he said that "God speaks . . . in a dream, in a vision of the night, / when deep sleep falls on mortals" (Job 33:14-15). Some people have intimations of God's nearness that prepare them for the message that shakes the soul, while for others the divine visitation comes without any apparent preparation.

I lay my odds that Joseph had some advance preparation. I don't mean that he was a bona fide mystic, but when I read that he was "a righteous man" I calculate that there was more to him than a run-of-the-mill soul.

But even if Joseph had some preparation for his dream, he had to be jolted when the angel addressed him as "Joseph, son of David." The last person in Joseph's family tree named David was King David. When the angel reached past Joseph's immediate father and several dozen other generations to connect him with his most famous ancestor, there had to be a reason. For one, though Joseph was now a village carpenter, he was part of the royal line.

This slight but powerful phrase might quicken Joseph to recall that when the Messiah would come, he would be a descendant of King David. And this would prepare Joseph to accept the fact that Mary's child was no ordinary child, and certainly no product of an illicit relationship or of a rape, but that the child had been "conceived . . . from the Holy Spirit" (Matthew 1:20). This was no ordinary baby. Now Joseph was instructed to take Mary to be his wife, no matter what people of the village might think, and to raise the child as though it were his own son.

Then God did a special favor for Joseph—a good thing, because Joseph was taking a rather thankless role—the angel told Joseph what the baby's name was to be, giving Joseph the privilege of naming him. I mention this because so often in biblical stories it was the mother who named the child. The baby was to have a special name, though at the time a relatively common one: name him *Jesus*, the angel said, because "he will save his people from their sins" (Matthew 1:21).

So it was that Joseph had a dream, and he acted on it. He took Mary as his wife and named the baby Jesus when he was born and began with Mary to watch over him.

Then, after some time, Joseph had another dream. After some wise men from the east sought out Jesus to pay him homage, the baby's life was in danger. So again "an angel of the Lord appeared to Joseph in a dream" (Matthew 2:13), and once again it was a succinct but crucial message. Joseph was to take the child and his mother and flee to Egypt, where they would be safe from King Herod's maniacal wrath.

That very night Joseph rose up and took his little family on the long, tedious journey to Egypt, where they remained until the death of Herod. Here was a strange, mini-version of history. Centuries earlier a teenage boy named Joseph had gone to Egypt as a slave, where eventually he saved his family and thousands of other persons from starvation. Now a young surrogate father named Joseph was taking his family to Egypt as refugees to save them from death by the hand of a tyrant king.

But Joseph the carpenter still wasn't done dreaming. When King Herod died, "an angel of the Lord suddenly appeared in a dream to Joseph in Egypt"(Matthew 2:19)—it's good, isn't it, that the angel had kept Joseph's forwarding address—and told him that those who were seeking the child's life were dead, so he could now return to his homeland. With that assuring word, Joseph moved the family to Nazareth where he and Mary raised Jesus and settled in to become part of the community that would eventually give Jesus his common, public name, Jesus of Nazareth.

As far as the Bible story is concerned, Joseph never dreamed again. Well, he probably had the kind of passing dreams that most of us have, those vignettes that are generally snippets of nothingness, though they may bless or startle us at the time. But Joseph never again had a dream that was recorded in the Bible. I suspect there was no need for any further dreaming on Joseph's part, because now he had fulfilled the crucial elements of his mission so that all that was left for him was the day-by-day responsibility of providing for his family and for watching the growth of this unique boy who was entrusted to his care. It's interesting that when Jesus, as a twelve-year-old, was separated from his family during a religious festival in Jerusalem, it is Mary who does the talking for the family, though Joseph clearly is there (Luke 2:41-51). But Joseph never appears in the story again.

You may remember that when I first began telling you this story about the Jewish parents who named their son Joseph, I said they had picked a good name because Joseph was one of the most revered persons in the history of their nation, Israel. That ancient Joseph, long ago, had been not only a heroic figure; more than that, he had played a key part in the founding of the nation of Israel and in saving the lives of thousands of people through his role as chief administrator under Pharaoh.

But I didn't mention another detail about the ancient Joseph, in a sense the most significant characteristic of this first holder of the name Joseph. This first Joseph was a dreamer too. A premier dreamer, in fact. If you remember your Sunday school stories, you'll recall that he had dreams that irritated his brothers to no end, dreams that got him in trouble so that his brothers sold him into slavery. And as a slave (indeed, as a jailbird) he interpreted dreams for two men—and as a result two years later he was given a chance to interpret dreams for Pharaoh, so that finally it was his gift for interpreting dreams that brought him to his eventual role as the key person in Pharaoh's cabinet.

So, many centuries later, when a Jewish family named their newborn son Joseph, I submit that they were wiser than they realized, because their son was a bigger and better dreamer than the first Joseph. I know, I know: the first Joseph dealt with dreams that saved the lives of thousands from starvation. But the young carpenter Joseph had three of the most important dreams in the history of the human race. The first persuaded him to stand by his fiancée, Mary, and authorized him to give the name *Jesus* to the baby that was to be born—and thus to identify Jesus as the Savior. The second dream saved the Baby's life. And the third dream saw to it that the Baby and his family got back to Israel where the rest of the plot was to unfold. And all of those dreams were short, direct, and businesslike: almost like a villager coming into the carpenter shop and saying, "I'd like a table—three cubits square and two cubits high—to be delivered in two weeks." No fanfare, no glamour, just the facts.

When we look back on history (especially sacred history) it's no doubt presumptuous to make judgments, but I'm going to venture one. I think that this second Joseph—the young carpenter—was a better, bigger, more sensitive dreamer than the Joseph who became prime minister of Egypt through his dreams. The first Joseph dreamed of his own success (honorable, of course, if it drives us to achievement), while the second Joseph dreamed of the success (if I may call it that) of his adopted son. The first Joseph told his dreams to his family, and later in interpretations to officers and the king; the second Joseph told his dreams to no one but his wife, Mary, but he carried them out with strength and dignity. The first Joseph saved the lives of thousands by interpreting Pharaoh's dreams. The second Joseph was, by his dreams, an agent in the salvation of humankind.

Haddon Chambers, the British dramatist, spoke of "the long arm of coincidence." It was a fascinating hour, centuries ago, when a Jewish family named their son Joseph in honor of a national hero known for his dreams. They could never have imagined that their son would become a better dreamer than his revered namesake.

CHAPTER NINE

THE LOVE STRATEGY

A mystery story doesn't have to include a love element, but it helps. If it is true, as it is famously and tiresomely said, that it's love that makes the world go around, then it's obvious that even a trivial, insubstantial love element adds luster to any story.

But when I speak of love and mystery in the same sentence, I realize that love itself is the ultimate mystery. We confess as much at an everyday, very pedestrian level on those rather frequent occasions when someone evaluates a marriage or romantic relationship with the intrusive idea, "I'll never understand what she sees in him." Love as observed from a distance (and sometimes as experienced in one's own life) is a mystery. There is no particular logic to it, not even when one of the parties is a professional logician. We smile understandingly when we say of the young that what they're experiencing is puppy love, but it's harder to explain when the subject is a very old dog.

But love is like that. Love is always quite mysterious, whether the love is that of romance, of family, of friendship, of school, or of country. More often than not we love first, then develop the rationale for it later. Love for family members or for institutions often grows over a long period of time, unlike the romantic experience that we describe as "falling in love," and yet even this nurtured love is often hard to explain. I love my hometown, even while admitting that I've seen numbers of towns more favorably situated. If I were to draw a profile of the most cherished friendships of my life, I wouldn't use that profile to find a new best friend. Those cherished friends got their role not by a list of qualifications but usually by some instinct beyond explaining. Probably someday, as scientists continue to unravel the mysteries of our genetic code they will give us a theory for why we love the persons we do. But if they do, pardon me; I won't believe them.

I say this because as I see it, this whole business of love has a quite irrational start. One of my favorite detectives, the Reverend Fleming Rutledge, writes, "The story of God and his world begins and comes to its consummation in his inexhaustible love."[1]

Let's look at the beginning. That most compelling and uniquely inspired storyteller, the author of Genesis, tells of the God who creates a universe so perfect that the Creator has to pause at intervals to rejoice in what is unfolding and to exclaim with almost childlike delight, "This is *good!*" It becomes clear that God's pleasure in this creation is not for selfish enjoyment. The Creator has put together this place of intricate engineering and exquisite beauty especially for the enjoyment of the human race.

But why? Why should God want to do something for the human race in general or for any combination of its particular parts? In our more cynical moments—or perhaps our more honest ones—most of us will confess that we've run into a fair number of human beings whom it's difficult to endure, let alone love. What made God love this human race?

James Weldon Johnson (1871–1938), the fine African American poet and for our purposes a good detective, in the poem "God's Trombones" portrays God stepping out into space and saying, *"I'm lonely — / I'll make me a world."* Then, with much of the wonder complete, God still feels lonely. God thinks about the problem and decides, "I'll make me a man!" It's a delightful picture, but strict theologians are of course uneasy with it because it implies that God is incomplete. On the other hand, perhaps it is the very completeness of God, as demonstrated in God's love, that compelled God to create a recipient for this divine love. What is love after all unless it has an object, a receiver? And even if the receiver rejects the offer, love has won—because love is complete in itself, once it is expressed. It is not destroyed simply because someone—or all the someones—has rejected it.

And as the biblical story reports it, we humans have done a pretty reckless artistic job of rejecting God's love. Philip Yancey, the contemporary Christian writer, says that the Bible is nothing other than the story of God, the jilted lover.[2]

It surely looks that way. The flora and fauna of Eden are hardly settled in place when the human race rejects the Giver in an irrational quest for what they think is going to be something still better, though the competing gift is quite ill-defined. And from that time forward humanity seems set on insulting God's love. When God presents a chosen people with a code of conduct (familiarly known as the Law, or the Ten Commandments) calculated to make their lives more orderly and fulfilling, they set out posthaste to break the code.

So how does God respond to this outrage? God responds like the love-struck teenager in stories from years past who comes with a new bouquet each day even though his intended rejects each previous gift. The Hebrew prophets had a good deal to say about this divine-human mismatch—especially the prophet Hosea. He became a kind of living object lesson of God's love as he married a woman who betrayed him after bearing several children before she eventually turns to a life of prostitution. Then, after losing her value in that market, she was at last being sold as a slave when Hosea found her again. He brought her home at God's command, providing a symbol of God's love for the nation of Israel: whatever their spiritual infidelities, no matter how often they might prostitute their faith with pagan gods, still God would pursue them, bring them home, make them his own again.

So God sums it up in this word to Hosea:

> When Israel was a child, I loved him,
>   and out of Egypt I called my son.
> The more I called them,
>   the more they went from me;
> they kept sacrificing to the Baals [the pagan gods],
>   and offering incense to idols.

But did God give up on such an ungracious people? Far from it!

> Yet it was I who taught Ephraim to walk,
>   I took them up in my arms;
>   but they did not know that I healed them.
> I led them with cords of human kindness,
>   with bands of love.
> I was to them like those
>   who lift infants to their cheeks.
> I bent down to them and fed them. (Hosea 11:1-4)

As the prophet Hosea comes to the end of his series of messages—each one seeming torn from his heart—he gives still one more call to the rebellious: "Return, O Israel, to the LORD your God." God continues to believe that there is something in this nation that will one day respond to the divine love: "I will heal their disloyalty; / I will love them freely" (Hosea 14:1, 4). God chooses through the prophet to portray his divine character as that of a foolish lover, never admitting that the scornful treatment may indeed be the true expression of the beloved's feelings—that perhaps this nation (or any given individual) is not worthy of love, and surely not of such reckless, profligate love that doesn't have the sense to know when it is being rejected and abused.

The New Testament turns the living parable of Hosea into a divine visitation. Now the goal is to win back not only the people of Israel but the whole human race. God chooses a mysterious—mysteriously illogical, at any rate—way of achieving the goal. A writer, whose capacity for mystery is so artful that he chooses the language of a philosopher, explains that in "the beginning" (by which pretty clearly he means the beginning of everything) there was "the Word" and that this Word "was with God . . . was God." Everything that exists came into being through this Word. Then, at some point in human history, this "Word became flesh and lived among us, and we have seen his glory, the glory as of a father's only son, full of grace and truth." Unfortunately, when he came into the world—this world that "came into being through him"—"the world did not know him." Indeed, he "came to what was his own, and his own people did not accept him." Those who did, however, gained the power to become children of God. (See John 1:1-14.)

What was the purpose of this divine visitation? We need to remind ourselves that this heavenly approach was made from a position of power—in truth, quite incalculable power—and basic logic says that where there is power, the aim is to use it. As the plot unfolds, however, this ultimate arsenal of power chooses to give up all the prerogatives of power. Another master of mystery writing, the man named Paul, says that this One who "was in the form of God" chose to empty himself of all this power in order to be "born in human likeness," accepting all the encumbrances of humanity, including the ultimate encumbrance of death itself—and no ordinary death at that but "even death on a cross" (Philippians 2:5-8).

Why? Why ever in the world would one follow a course so diametrically opposed to all that is reasonable? Our culture recommends, if you have power, flaunt it. Why, instead, would one choose to abdicate this power and thus make oneself the willing victim of an enemy's power, thus accepting an execution in the form developed to bring the ultimate in both suffering and humiliation? We need to remind ourselves that crucifixion was not simply a way to punish crime or to rid society of its miscreants. It was calculated to make death as lingering as possible, in the degradation of helpless nudity in a public place, thus to make this person a nonperson—someone whose only value is in being displayed as having no value. This was the way of death for One who was "equal with God" and who would not otherwise have to undergo death in even its most gracious form.

This takes us back to our other master of mystery, John, who puts it simply, directly, and unforgettably: "For God so loved the world that he gave his only Son, so that everyone who believes in him may not perish but may have eternal life" (John 3:16). We're back to that mystery of love. As we said earlier, love often is a mystery; in most instances we try to establish a case for its logic after we are already taken by it. But never more so than in this story.

Now let's try for a minute to see what's going on. God is seeking to do business with this human race to which originally he gave, for no payment whatsoever, a universe of unutterable beauty and resources—resources so vast that I suspect most are still undiscovered. The human race, *noblesse oblige,* has on the whole treated this generosity with varying degrees of disinterest and abuse, thanking whatever gods they may know only in cases when they fear they may lose some of these favors. So how shall God win back this people who seem generally so mindless of divine love?

It's quite simple. God says, "I will love them still more." But how to love them still more when already they have been given so much? Again, it's quite simple: show them love in the most dramatic form by becoming one of them and going to death on their behalf. In the words of the mystery writer I quoted a few moments ago, "Rarely will anyone die for a righteous person—though perhaps for a good person someone might actually dare to die. But God proves his love for us in that while we still were sinners Christ died for us" (Romans 5:7-8). It was while "we were enemies" of

God that "we were reconciled to God through the death of his Son" (Romans 5:10).

Obviously, this scenario is not simply a mystery; it violates common sense as we know it. And yet, to put it pragmatically, it's good if it works.

And therein lies the further indignity in the story. God's act of love is a complete gamble. There is no promise that God's plan will work, no obligation on humanity's part to respond positively. Come to think of it, with humanity's record for rational response, the odds in God's favor seem poor indeed.

Nearly two thousand years have now passed since God's ultimate venture of love, the venture that began at Bethlehem and climaxed at Calvary. We have no authoritative scorekeeper who can evaluate the scene with a measure of accuracy, but from all one can see God hasn't come out very well. It looks as though most of the human race continues to ignore God except when something goes wrong on the planet—not only some large-scale disaster such as a tsunami but even the individual troubles that occur for most of us at one time or another, in which case almost everyone becomes a theologian and accuses God of neglecting this admirable human race.

It seems rather clear that our human race doesn't think about God too often, except on rare occasions of spiritual sensitivity—or on the other hand, of the kind of angry questioning to which I have just referred.

There are, however, those remarkable individuals whom we call *saints*. Some of them are officially canonized by bodies of believers, but almost all of us have inducted one or several persons into such recognition on the basis of our own judgment. Organized religion has been very astute in including in its calendar a day known as All Saints' Day to acknowledge that there are—and always have been—saints among us who are not widely known but who are as worthy of the title as anyone officially named by an ecclesiastical body.

And how do we recognize such persons? What is the job description for a saint or the pattern of conduct by which the rest of us mortals might identify them? In a word, by the way such persons show love for others. That is, we know a saint because saints are like God: they love when there is no benefit to them in doing so, indeed in many instances when their love is abused. Saints give themselves in loving service to the deserving and to the undeserving, to the grateful and to the indifferent, to those who are themselves so attractive that one feels rewarded simply by their attractiveness and also to persons so unattractive in person or response that love itself seems somehow sullied by having been invested in them.

But this, after all, is the way God has loved, so it is a good standard by which to determine what constitutes a saint, the kind of person who has drawn close enough to God and is enough captured by God's Spirit to reflect even in a measure the character of God. And it seems clear that those who follow such a way of life—those people that most of us see as saints—are quite surely a minority in our world. One might think therefore that God has to be disappointed that such a small number choose so to live. But Jesus indicated that God finds pleasure in even such a limited response. Jesus said that the Kingdom of God is like a tiny bit of leaven, so small in itself yet powerful enough to leave its influence in the whole lump. And again, Jesus says that God's kingdom is like a grain of mustard seed, something so insignificant that it can easily be lost in a crack of the hand, yet powerful far beyond its size.

This, I suspect, is consistent with God's whole strategy of love. Most of the time love is not a massive marching band but a quiet piccolo; it is not an army that invades our planet but a Baby's cry at Bethlehem. Love is a Body bleeding in shame at Calvary, not a dictator strutting his power.

But a realist is not satisfied. Isn't there some better strategy? By definition God has all power at reach; isn't there some method or energy or compulsion more effective than love? The answer? No, not if we want God to maintain the character that Jesus Christ declared God to have.

But our realist has one more question. Will love win? In a planet so badly disarrayed as ours, will love win?

I believe it will. Indeed, I'm altogether sure that love will win—God's love, that is, and all the love that flows from it. But of course it's by faith that I've come to this conclusion, and I can't prove it.

But so what? I told you that love is a mystery.

CHAPTER TEN

TIME. AND TIME AGAIN.

Time is a factor in every mystery story. If murder is suspected, the coroner is asked to identify the time of death as well as the means. When suspects are interviewed, there's an early question: "Where were you between (say) midnight and 1:00 a.m.? Was anyone with you who can verify that time?" Extended periods of time are often as important as specific times. "How long did you know the victim?" "How long were you employed by Jones and Brown?" Time is always important. Before we carried it on our wrist, in a BlackBerry, or in our pocket, before Big Ben chimed out its passing, and before there were sundials—time has always mattered to us human beings.

But of course time is more than a factor in mystery stories. Time itself is a mystery. It's one of the world's deepest mysteries, Eric D. Carlson says. I think time fascinates us because we know it (and intuit it) at two quite different levels. On the one hand, we sense that we have a limited supply of time, which at intervals drives us to hurry because we know we're moving steadily, day after day, to the end of our personal supply of this unique, limited resource. On the other hand, something in us knows that we are eternal creatures. We sense that something in us—the something that is the real us—is going to go on, because something in us is beyond time. Perhaps the ultimate reason limited time matters to us is because we have this instinct for the unlimited.

That remarkable book the Bible understands our compelling sense of time—understands it so well, in fact, that it introduces time on the first page and exits with it on the last. Indeed, in one major English translation the last word, except for the benediction, is *soon*, which is a pretty timely word (Revelation 22:20).

"In the beginning," says the writer of Genesis, and then to let our mortal minds grasp the unfolding scenario he tells the story over a period of seven days. *Days* I can grasp. Eons and cesium (which can vibrate 9,192,631,770 times a second) are quite beyond my grasp. So I like it when Genesis talks about days, and I don't really care too much whether the writer was speaking mathematically or poetically, I'm just grateful that he chose to use a word I am able to wrap my mind around.

The writer of Genesis did something more. He comforted me with the impression that God, who clearly needs no timepiece, accommodates us by dealing with time on our terms. True, one of the psalmists says that a thousand years in God's sight "are like yesterday when it is past, / or like a watch in the night" (Psalm 90:4), but he still keeps his figure of speech in words and concepts that are familiar to me.

But always time matters to the biblical writers. God walks in the garden "at the time of the evening breeze" (Genesis 3:8), and when the writer says it, the clock in my soul registers with him. We know next to nothing about some early personalities, but we know how old they were when their first sons were born and how old they were when they died. Abraham is the key transition figure in what we sometimes call "salvation history," and we know how old he was when God spoke to him in a decisive way, how old he was when his sons were born, and how old he was when he died. The life of Moses, the transmitter of the Law and the liberator of Israel, is divided into three equal parts of forty years each; and even as we read that, we remember that *forty* is a quasi-mystical number in the Bible with significance beyond the quantity factor. This is important, because all of us know that time is like that. It is in its own right so ordinary that every human gets the same amount on any given day: no one is so rich, so wise, so creative as to get more moments in a day than the most desultory, the most indifferent, the most wicked. So the numbers of life carry more than can be quantified, and we understand why the Hebrews attached mystical significance to numbers.

The great Hebrew prophets had a particular perception of time. They knew that no deed is confined to the hour in which it is performed; good or bad, the deed reaches beyond the present. So the prophets thundered mightily about what persons or nations do now, because now is soon tomorrow and what I do now draws the profile of tomorrow. Sometimes, it seems to me, this sense gave prophets a kind of double vision, by which they might speak to an issue in the immediate and impose upon it or stretch back of it something generations or centuries removed. So Isaiah writes to his beleaguered time, "The people who walked in darkness / have seen a great light; / those who lived in a land of deep darkness — / on them light has shined," then goes on to promise that a day is coming when a child will be born whose name will be "Everlasting Father, Prince of Peace" (Isaiah 9:2, 6). The prophet seemed to look at one time, the time almost in reach, then see it superimposed on a future time and swallowed up by it. Very possibly he was speaking a word for his generation, but ever since the first century the church has believed that he was speaking to the birth of the Messiah, as well, even though the Messiah came hundreds of years after Isaiah's vision.

So, more and more, a quality of expectation came to impregnate the thinking of the Hebrew prophets—those extraordinary detectives!—as they looked at time. Time became for them a tapestry of hope. Mind you, the immediate stuff of the tapestry might be dark beyond description, but because of their hope-orientation they could construct scenes of unrealistic beauty. So Isaiah says: "They shall beat their swords into plowshares, / and their spears into pruning hooks; / nation shall not lift up sword against nation, / neither shall they learn war any more" (Isaiah 2:4). Isaiah may have seen this when nations were in an armaments race (such exercises have gone on for millennia) or perhaps in a time of diplomatic lassitude with no impossible dreamer on the scene. No matter. For the prophets, time was not a flatland; it was a rising range of hope.

And more and more the center of that hope was a coming King, a Messiah. He would be God's gift not only for Israel but through Israel for the whole world and with a reign that would know no end.

But the time would have to be right. It would have to be the intersection where time on the calendar—the kind of time with which historians do business—would intersect with time in the arena of divine purpose and redemption.

And it wasn't just the Hebrew prophets who were doing a detective job with time. William Barclay says that "the strange thing is that, just about the time when Jesus was born, there was in the world a strange feeling of expectation, a waiting for the coming of a king." Barclay spreads his evidence: writings from what we might call secular prophets and from a variety of cultures in the general period in which Jesus was born, such as the Roman historians Suetonius and Tacitus; Josephus, the Jewish historian; and Virgil, the Roman poet—each of them examining the edges of extraordinary expectation.[1]

The Apostle Paul looked back on the event of Jesus' coming perhaps thirty years after the death and resurrection of Jesus Christ and was struck by the timeliness of it all. He was, of course, an exceptionally qualified detective, because he was a student of both the Hebrew prophets and the great secular poets and philosophers of the Greeks and the Romans. Putting together his evidence, Paul said that "God sent his Son" at "the fullness of time" (Galatians 4:4). The time was uniquely right—or perhaps we would say that the time was *ripe*.

Ancient astronomers would have imagined a perfect constellation of the stars. Take away their idea that the stars controlled human destinies and you are left nevertheless with a wonderfully dramatic picture of the timeliness of what happened; it was as though all of the universe had to be rightly aligned for a moment of such significance as this—for the occasion of a birth in a Judean village to a teenage Gallilean girl. To put the image in another metaphor, a playful one, I think of the concert-goer who was fascinated by the role within the symphony of the person who manned the cymbals. "What," he asked, "do you have to know in order to play the cymbals?" The musician replied, "You have to know *when.*"

That's what Paul saw in the birth of the Christ: a *whenness.* It's our natural, logical inclination to look at the economic, political, religious, military, and sociological data of the world at that point—something over two thousand years ago—and to make of this data a configuration of perfection, the fullness of time. And I suspect there's something admirable about our attempt, something like the medieval village piper who did the best he could to welcome the king and queen when they came through his town in a once-in-a-century event. But it still manages only a small, earnest portion of what the apostle seemed to feel.

As I see it, the only other detective who got the idea that Saint Paul had in mind was the holy genius who gave us the Gospel of John. He was obsessed with time, whatever the level of its domain. He opens his book like a philosopher who is waving excitedly at something he hardly dares put in words. "In the beginning was the Word, and the Word was with God, and the Word was God" (John 1:1). We know that it's no accident that John chooses to begin with the same language as the Genesis creation story, because John wants us to know that even at the creation God was thinking of the redemption of the human race. At this point John deals with time like a poet and a philosopher, in a style that can challenge the best talents in both fields.

But John also is time-conscious when dealing with the most routine matters. When he begins telling us of Jesus' activities, he gives us a timetable that is matter of fact yet specific: "The next day" (1:29), "The next day" (1:35), "The next day" (1:43). In stories that might seem to be made up of quite ordinary parts, John interrupts to tell us the time. So when two of the first followers of Jesus have their first extended conversation with the Teacher, John finishes that part of the story, "It was about four o'clock in the afternoon" (1:39). He bothers to give us the time partly because he is an artist-storyteller who wants us to be equally attentive readers so we will whisper to ourselves, "It was a time never to be forgotten," and partly because he simply is captured by the peculiar significance of time.

So, too, when John tells the story of Nicodemus, a Pharisee who dared to seek out Jesus for a private interview, he bothers to include this detail: "He came to Jesus by night" (John 3:2). A casual reader will say, "So what?" A scholar will tell us that in the Jewish world most dedicated students did their research by night. A certain kind of psychologist will say that Nicodemus was coming when no one would see him. A poet will smile, thoughtfully: "John wants us to know that Nicodemus is living in the dark. For Nicodemus it would have been *night* even if he had come at noonday."

John exercises the same mood near the end of the drama, when Jesus dismisses his betrayer, Judas. John tells us, as Judas leaves the meeting room, "And it was night" (John 13:30). A matter of fact reader might rightly say, "Of course it was night. They were eating their supper." The poet, again, sees something more: for Judas this is more than an hour on the clock; this is his entry into the utter darkness of the human soul.

But John's absorption with time comes to its most exquisite expression when he deals with time in Jesus' life—specifically, when an hour on the clock (or a watch in the night, in biblical language) most clearly intersects with eternity. Or to put it another way, when a common moment is made eternally uncommon by what in God's plan is un-folding at that moment.

This is where the biblical scholars join our detective team. Good scholars are always detectives, of course; they spend their hours seeking one more piece of evidence to prove a point or a piece to disprove what some other scholar has said. They don't have much to do with pathol-ogists, but they often call in archaeologists, who are in some sense first cousins of pathologists.

One of the best scholar-detectives on the subject of time was a German theologian, Oscar Cullmann. As you've often heard, "the Greeks have a word for it" (for almost everything, that is), and so it is with *time*. They gave us *chronos*, for example, from which we get our word *chrono-logical*. This is the kind of time we measure with clock or calendar. And *aion*, which means an extended period of time, what we would call an *age*, as when a historian refers to a period as "the Victorian age." And then there's *kairos*, which means "a point in time"—the kind of time made his-toric during World War II when military leaders spoke of "D-day," which was not simply a date on the calendar (though of course it was that), but more particularly a day absolutely crucial to their battle plans, a day on which his-tory would balance precariously.

So Professor Cullmann points us to a day when the brothers of Jesus—who at that time did not believe in him—chided Jesus for not going to Jerusalem for a particu-lar festival. Jesus answered, "My *kairos* [to go up to Jerusalem] has not yet come; your *kairos* is always ready." Jesus' brothers could go to Jerusalem at any time, because their *kairoi* depended entirely on their own human deci-sions. Not so for Christ; "he stands in the midst of the di-vine plan of salvation, whose *kairoi* are definitely fixed by God."[2]

And when Jesus was crucified, he spoke a time-word with the *kairos* quality. John puts it this way: "He said, 'It is finished.' Then he bowed his head and gave up his spirit"

(John 19:30). *Finished.* The assigned task is complete, so now Jesus is read to "give up his spirit"—as if, his work done, Jesus was giving himself permission to die. His time had come. His next *kairos* would come on Easter morning, "while it was still dark" (John 20:1).

I can't leave this time matter in its *kairos* quality without getting personal about it. I'm thinking about the daily business of life as you and I experience it—I mean the stuff that ordinarily makes up our *chronos*—and where the wonder of *kairos* might touch it. This is the mood that drove the Apostle Paul. "See then that ye walk circumspectly, not as fools, but as wise, Redeeming the time, because the days are evil" (Ephesians 5:15-16 KJV). The apostle—a careful handler of the Greek—uses the word *kairos* for time. It's as though he were urging believers to take the predictable minutiae of their days, the basic element available to every human being, and make *kairos* of it.

But of course! If one believes that any day, any hour intersects with eternity, then there is a *kairos* quality to every day. If it be true that God has a purpose in our lives, then who can estimate when that purpose may manifest itself in some memorable way? "Do not neglect to show hospitality to strangers," a New Testament writer advised, "for by doing that some have entertained angels without knowing it" (Hebrews 13:2). To put it in the language of time, who knows what *kairos* moments come our way in any given week only to be lost by our insensitivity—that is, by seeing them only in a *chronos* way. I suspect that we are often so taken with the immediate that we miss the eternal—so preoccupied with the *chronos* of our date book, our BlackBerry, our wristwatch that we miss the shattering beauty of our *kairos,* a spectacular moment when eternity seeks our attention.

This is to say that time is, indeed, a mystery. Because there's time. And then, again, there's *time.*

CHAPTER ELEVEN

THE MAN OF OPPORTUNITY

When the entertainment industry gives out its annual awards they always include recognition for the best supporting actor or actress. This is not the person on whom the camera is most frequently focused, but without this person the major focus might not matter. Some of these supporting characters are part of the story from the beginning, while others enter—often inauspiciously—along the way or even near the end.

I'm thinking of two stories just now—two stories with parallel plots. Each one had a key supporting actor; one is completely anonymous and the other is infamously known. Come to think of it, the lead character in the first story is also unknown, while the lead in the later story is without doubt the best-known name in human history. But forgive me; I'm getting ahead of myself.

The people of Israel—the people who under God gave us the Hebrew Scriptures that we call the Old Testament—took sin seriously. They worried about it. This makes them rather different from us. We avoid mentioning the word, though we have developed an elaborate system of synonyms, most of them appropriate to given fields. Where the Israelites spoke of sin, we speak of *mistakes*. When committed by someone else we may declare it a *serious mistake*.

In the world of business it is sometimes *poor judgment*, and a really serious business person may even refer to it as *an ethical lapse*. For ourselves or for our good friends, we find professional language: it isn't a matter of sin but perhaps a *psychological predisposition* or *an unfortunate family trait*.

But the Israelites, I repeat, took sin seriously. This is because they took God seriously. Thus a man cried out to God in one of the most poignant prayers of all time,

> Against you, you alone, have I sinned,
>   and done what is evil in your sight,
> so that you are justified in your sentence
>   and blameless when you pass judgment. (Psalm 51:4)

However God might choose to punish this man, this man sees God as justified in doing so. That's how serious he is about sin.

Since that was the case, the biggest day of the year in Israel was not New Year's Day or Thanksgiving Day but the Day of Atonement. This was the day when the nation dealt, at a national level, with sin. One might appear before God as an individual sinner at any time, but the Day of Atonement was a national act of repentance.

The day was full of ceremony and ritual, all of it dramatic in symbolism. Some of its details in its ancient form would be a bit difficult for most of our modern sensibilities. It's interesting that we are more comfortable with heinous sin (as evidenced by our readiness to hear it reported on the evening news) than with graphic atonement for sin.

I want us to concentrate on one peculiar activity of the Day of Atonement. Early in the ritual the high priest would take a bull and two goats. The bull and one goat were slain, and their blood was sprinkled ceremoniously, seven times, on the mercy seat of the altar in their place of worship. This brought atonement for the holy place, the tent of meeting, and the altar.

Then the high priest, in his epic moment of the year, was to

> lay both his hands on the head of the live goat, and confess over it all the iniquities of the people of Israel, and all their transgressions, all their sins, putting them on the head of the goat, and sending it away into the wilderness by means of someone designated for the task. The goat shall bear on itself all their iniquities to a barren region; and the goat shall be set free in the wilderness. (Leviticus 16:21-22)

Even if you aren't a conventionally religious person you can appreciate the symbolic drama of the day. The idea has appeared in its basic outline in many different forms among many peoples. In some ancient island cultures the natives would place symbolic objects in a boat, then watch the boat slip out to sea. When the boat was out of sight, they felt they were free of the particular curse. In some other cultures, symbols of sickness would be laid upon an animal and the animal would be driven into the wilderness. In still other cultures, some token of a sickness or disaster would be placed on a human being, and that person might be beaten or killed with the thought that if that person or animal "carried away" the sickness or the tragedy the rest of the tribe would be spared.

But the Israelites, I repeat, were a remarkable people. They didn't seek simply to have their troubles or their sickness or some natural disaster carried away but their *sins*. They wanted to know that their relationship to God was without impediment, and they understood that sin was ultimately the basis for all of earth's pain—most particularly because sin separates the human soul from God. The primary issue, therefore, was to be rid of sin. And because they had a sense of community, of human solidarity, which is difficult for people of our individualistic culture to understand, they sought forgiveness not for their personal sins but for the sins of the nation.

Who was the *Azazel* to whom the goat was sent? For this I turn to one of my favorite detectives, Professor Robert

Alter, a scholar whom I honor not only for his knowledge of Hebrew and of the Hebrew Scriptures but also for his feeling for literature. He suggests that the ritual rests upon a polarity between the Lord God and the pale of human civilization on the one hand, and Azazel and "the realm of disorder and raw formlessness" (symbolized by the remote wilderness) on the other. "It is as though the goat piled with impurities were being sent back to the primordial realm of 'welter and waste' before the delineated world came into being, but that realm here is given an animal-or-demon tag." Dr. Alter notes further that early rabbis added to the momentum of the ritual by imagining the goat being pushed off a high cliff.[1] But the descriptive word in Leviticus is simply that the animal was set free in the howling wilderness, far from human habitation—a place, I suspect, that most humans avoided even in the daylight hours—a place they saw as the realm of Azazel, of lostness and desolation.

That goat has gotten a place not only in our religious consciousness but even in our language. The dictionary calls him the *scapegoat,* with the definition, "one who is made to bear the blame for others or to suffer in their place." The dictionary then directs its readers to the biblical incident we've described.[2] Our common speech has abbreviated the term. Thus we say of a person who is easily victimized, "Poor soul! She always ends up being the *goat.*" Or someone says of himself in a mood of self-pity, "Wherever I go, I seem to be the goat." When next you hear the term, picture a beast being led into the wilderness in the ancient Middle East.

But if the scapegoat was the lead character—albeit an unknowing one—in the long ago celebration of the Day of Atonement, I want us to observe now the supporting character, the man who led the goat into the wilderness, perhaps even to a cliff—perhaps, in such a scenario, even pushing the animal off the cliff. His assignment doesn't seem to call for any unique skill. He needed to be familiar enough with animal life to cope with the peculiar personality of the goat, but in a pastoral economy almost any teenage boy or girl had such experience. The person needed enough courage to go at least to the edge of the wilderness, and more likely into the wilderness itself, to set the goat on its course of lostness. Yes, and courageous enough to deal if necessary with wild beasts along the way. But on the whole, it doesn't seem to have been a skilled job. One assumes that hundreds of men would be qualified to take it on.

Perhaps. But one gets the feeling that this person was nevertheless quite special. We're not told how he was chosen, which only adds to his mystery, but it's clear that he was seen as being out of the ordinary. The New Revised Standard Version of the Bible calls him "someone designated for the task," then adds in a footnote, "Meaning of Hebrew uncertain" (Leviticus 16:21). If you're a detective, it's hard to let that one go. The ace detective to whom I referred earlier, Robert Alter, calls him "a man for the hour" and explains in his footnote that the "expression appears only here" and that its literal sense is "a timely man," and that "it probably indicates a man chosen to serve for this time and task."[3]

But I like best of all the language of the King James Version, the translation in which I first read the Bible as a boy. Here he is called "a fit man," with the footnote, "Hebrew, a man of opportunity." Whenever you think of this anonymous character—background unidentified, training unknown, yet trusted with a uniquely sacred assignment—call him "a man of opportunity." He is only a supporting actor in the drama of a nation's redemption—some would even identify him, I suppose, as a bit player—but as he walks along, sometimes prodding his reluctant companion, doing what is surely unskilled labor, know that for this year a nation's sense of divine acceptance rests upon his doing his peculiarly ordinary task successfully.

I said at the outset, however, that I was going to tell two stories. I'm led into the second story by the unidentified person who gave us the New Testament book of Hebrews. Let me remind you that all of the New Testament writers were sacred detectives. They were persons who loved the Hebrew Scriptures; all of them except Luke had known these Scriptures from their youth and understood them to be the word of God and therefore the surest hope of the human race in general and of the people of Israel in particular. Now, having come to know Jesus of Nazareth as the Christ and as the living Word of God, they found in the Hebrew Scriptures all kinds of truth they had never known before. So it is that so often they preface or complete their reporting of some event in the life of Jesus by saying something like, "All this took place to fulfill what had been spoken by the Lord through the prophet" (Matthew 1:22).

The detective work in the book of Hebrews goes beyond all the rest. He (or perhaps she; some say it might have been Priscilla) found pictures of Christ not only in the messages of the prophets but also in numbers of places, events, rituals, and ceremonies of the Hebrew Scriptures. So when the writer refers to the sacrifice that Jesus made at Calvary he sees significance in the place of our Lord's death. "For the bodies of those animals whose blood is brought into the sanctuary by the high priest as a sacrifice for sin are burned outside the camp. Therefore Jesus also suffered outside the city gate in order to sanctify the people by his own blood" (Hebrews 13:11-12).

The writer of Hebrews was dealing with an idea that many of the early scholars of the church, such as Leo the Great in the fifth century, pondered. Jesus was the ultimate sacrifice, yet it was not on an altar in the place of worship; rather, he died in a public place on a public highway outside the city, so to speak. Thus his death had its symbolism in the disposal of the animal sacrifices in a place of burning outside the city. But there is a picture, too, in the scapegoat, because it died not at the altar of the temple but outside the city—indeed, outside civilization, much as one would treat a shameful criminal, a creature so rep-rehensible that it was better it should be banished from public view.

But I am more interested still in how Jesus got to the place of death. I reason that there must be a supporting actor, someone like that "man for the hour," or even more particularly, "the man of opportunity."

I offer two possibilities—two quite different possibili-ties, in fact. The first is the man named Judas. He was one of the twelve disciples, the chosen group privileged to live with Jesus day after day, observe his miracles, bathe in his teachings and in the wonder of his person. I suspect that he was in many ways one of the most talented of the dis-ciples. I judge this from his being chosen to serve as the group's treasurer. After all, several of the disciples were small business owners, part of family fishing businesses that had additional employees; and Matthew was a tax col-lector, accustomed to handling money. Yet Judas was the treasurer of the twelve. There had to have been a good ar-gument for his being chosen above his fellows.

But something went wrong in Judas's soul, so wrong that eventually he betrayed his Lord for thirty pieces of sil-ver. The Gospel of John indicates that he did so out of his love of money. Some scholars, wanting to redeem Judas's name, try to prove that Judas was very committed to Jesus as a political redeemer and that he hoped that by the be-trayal he would force Jesus to declare himself as Israel's king. However it was, Judas betrayed Jesus.

Having made his betrayal contract with the enemies of Jesus, Judas had to find the circumstance that was just right: an occasion when there was the least danger of people ris-ing up to defend Jesus. The Gospels of Matthew and Luke use the same phrase to describe what was going on in Judas's mind: he "began to look for an opportunity to betray him" (Matthew 26:16, Luke 22:6).

The phrase intrigues me because it reminds me of that phrase that the King James Version says best expresses the

Hebrew description for the man who took the scapegoat into the wilderness: he was "a man of opportunity."

I'm not trying to establish a doctrine. I'm just a detective, that's all, and I find it fascinating that the man who led the scapegoat on the Day of Atonement was a man of opportunity—and that when Judas agreed to betray Jesus, he set out immediately to find the opportunity to do so.

The other possibility is a man who was somewhere in the crowd on the day Jesus was being led to crucifixion. His name was Simon, and he was from Cyrene on the North African coast. Here is Mark's report: "They compelled a passer-by, who was coming in from the country, to carry his cross; it was Simon of Cyrene, the father of Alexander and Rufus" (Mark 15:21). Careful students have long suggested that when Mark bothers to tell us that Simon is the father of Alexander and Rufus it indicates that these men were well-known as early followers of Jesus. Some note that the Apostle Paul includes a Rufus in his list of greetings when he writes to the church at Rome (Romans 16:13).

So perhaps Simon the Cyrenian is the man of opportunity. After all, he was just in town, probably doing routine business, when Roman soldiers rudely pulled him—by chance?—from his place as an innocent bystander and made him Jesus' companion, carrying our Lord's cross outside the town to the place of crucifixion. Was it divine providence that Simon was standing just where he was at just the opportune time?

So I'm watching two scenes today. Very, very long ago the people of Israel chose a man of opportunity to guide the scapegoat into the wilderness as he carried, by their faith, the nation's sins of the year. And now I see a day almost two millennia ago when another Scapegoat carried the sins, not simply of a nation but of all humankind, and not simply for a year but for the ages, to a place outside the city. And here again, I see an opportune figure. Is it Judas the betrayer, or is it Simon the bearer of the cross? Or is it both, like all the mixed figures of our human race?

CHAPTER TWELVE

BEHOLD, THE LAMB!

If a lamb is part of a mystery story, you can be sure that the lamb is the victim and not the perpetrator. It's hard to think of anything a lamb might kill. A ram can take care of itself pretty well, but a lamb is the quintessential victim. And I promise that while a storyteller has a right to demonstrations of perversity in the way that he or she deals with characters and while I confess that I'm not above such an occasional twist, I don't intend to surprise you with a perverse personality for the lamb.

It's interesting to see how prominent the lamb is in the Bible. You'll find this helpless creature roughly two hundred times in the Old and New Testaments. Compare that with the lion (with all its standing as king of the beasts) or cattle or even sheep, and you have to wonder how such an unlikely little creature as the lamb has won so much attention. It's easy to understand why the biblical poets would pay attention to the half-mythological leviathan of the sea, or the lion that was ready to devour—or, at quite the other extreme, the locusts who by their sheer numbers could wipe out a harvest and all promise of life. But a *lamb?* When one thinks of a lamb, one thinks of helplessness and gentleness— a creature dependent on the mercy and attentiveness of stronger creatures. This idea is written into our oldest rhythmic childhood memories: "Mary had a little lamb"— and into proverbs dating back at least to the seventh century, when some unknown soul promised that God "tempers the wind to the shorn lamb."

If you think, as I suggested at the outset, that a lamb is going to be a victim, you're right. But if that's all you think, you're wrong.

It's a long story, but I'll try to keep it short. The first clue in the record of the lamb comes in one of the most penetrating stories in all of literature, but before I deal with it let me mention a faux clue from the Garden of Eden. After Adam and Eve have sinned they realize that they are naked, and they cover themselves with fig leaves. But God, after confronting them concerning their conduct, "made garments of skins for the man and for the woman, and clothed them" (Genesis 3:21). Some detectives working this story insist that the skins must have come from a lamb. This adds intrigue to the role of the lamb, but it's not a provable point, and our story is good enough in its own right that we don't have to bolster it with an interesting theory that lacks any real evidence.

But go with me now as the biblical plot unfolds, to the story of Abraham and Sarah. They have a miracle son, through whose line "all the families of the earth shall be blessed" (Genesis 12:3). But when this son, Isaac, is at the least a robust teenager and possibly a young man, Abraham is instructed to sacrifice him. It is the kind of story that should be told with violins, oboes, flutes, and French horns playing in the background, as an aged father takes a lonely journey to the place where he has been told to sacrifice "your son, your only son Isaac, whom you love" (Genesis 22:2). Somewhere in the epochal three-day journey, Isaac speaks: "Father. . . . The fire and the wood are here, but where is the lamb for a burnt offering?" To which Abraham replies, "God himself will provide the lamb for a burnt offering, my son." The writer concludes the scene with the same words with which he began it: "So the two of them walked on together" (Genesis 22:6-8).

Just when the father is about to strike the fatal blow to his son, "the angel of the Lord called to him," instructing him not to lay a hand on his son. Abraham has passed the test of obedience. As Abraham "looked up," he "saw a ram, caught in a thicket by its horns" (Genesis 22:13). Abraham had expected a lamb—an indication, beyond doubt, that lambs were at the time the usual animal of ritual sacrifice. There's a certain kind of natural logic in this, because a lamb seems the best symbol of purity among mammals, just as does the dove among birds. Abraham seems to have gone to the mount of sacrifice with his son expecting that God would, in time, provide a lamb. Or is it, perhaps, that Abraham chose to see his son as the essence of a helpless lamb, beautiful and pure and willing to allow his father to bind him to an altar of death? No one can say, but this we know for sure: Abraham conceived of a lamb as the essential sacrifice, and he was confident that, however the story might unfold, the lamb would be God's own provision. And for the particular quality of the remarkable Abraham-Isaac story, remember the specific source of Abraham's confidence: "*God himself* will provide the lamb for a burnt offering, my son" (italics added).

The unique place of the lamb in biblical significance is defined ineradicably in the book of Exodus, as the nation of Israel comes to birth and escapes the slavery of Egypt. This story gives a crucible of language and concepts still celebrated millennia later by both Jews and Christians.

For Jews, the occasion is the Passover. On the night when the Israelites were to march from Egypt to freedom, Moses told them that a death angel would pass through the land, claiming the firstborn of man and beast. Those who believed Moses' words were to take a lamb "without blemish, a year old male," one for a family—and if a household was too small, they were to join with the closest neighbor. Blood from the lamb was to be put on the two doorposts and the lintel of each house. Then the family would eat the lamb, "roasted over the fire with unleavened bread and bitter herbs" (Exodus 12:7-8). Moses promised the people that the death angel would pass over the houses where the blood of the lamb was sprinkled as commanded.

The sacrificial lamb has been part of the story of the Jewish and Christian faiths ever since. More than eighty times in Exodus, Leviticus, and Numbers lambs are specifically referred to in the ritual instructions. When the prophet Isaiah describes the suffering of God's chosen representative, he identifies him as "like a lamb that is led to the slaughter," a creature that is "silent . . . did not open his mouth" (Isaiah 53:7).

But the story takes a peculiar turn in the New Testament. For several years the dynamic, somewhat enigmatic preacher, John the Baptist, had taught and preached in the wilderness. As he preached, the crowds grew, and so did their questions. Who was this exotic preacher? And particularly, was he perhaps the Messiah for whom they had waited so long? John brushed the question aside, insisting that he was simply a forerunner, assigned to prepare the way for the greater one who was to follow. Then one day John "saw Jesus coming toward him and declared, 'Here is the Lamb of God who takes away the sin of the world'" (John 1:29).

Underline those few words as the most remarkable nominating speech of human history. John the Baptist has seen the presentation of the Messiah as his life's calling; indeed, on the basis of the story in Luke 1 we may assume that his parents told him he was born for such a task as this. He has gladly shrugged off what must have been frequent attempts to put the spotlight on him rather than on the person he would eventually introduce. He has told his inquirers that the person for whom he was preparing the way was of such quality that he, John, wasn't worthy to untie his sandals. And when at last he introduces Jesus— obviously the person he has said he was waiting for—he identifies him as "the Lamb of God who takes away the sin of the world." This must have seemed an unlikely description to people who were anticipating a messianic deliverer.

There is more. In early statements about this one who was to come, John described him as a commanding, quite terrifying figure: "His winnowing fork is in his hand, and he will clear his threshing floor and will gather his wheat into the granary; but the chaff he will burn with unquenchable fire" (Matthew 3:12). So when John presents this personality of judgment and fire, he calls him *the Lamb of God*. What figures?

Later detectives who have worked the story only add to our marveling. Richard Crashaw lived barely thirty-six years (1613–1649), but left behind some magnificent poetry. Poets are especially good detectives, of course, because poets insist on looking beneath the surface of all they see. So, using John the Baptist's language to look at Christ, Crashaw wrote in "The Dear Bargain":

> What did the Lamb that He should die?
> What did the Lamb that He should need
> When the wolf sins, Himself to bleed?

How indeed is it that the Lamb dies for the wolf's conduct? Why is the Lamb's blood shed for the creature that causes bloodshed?

You see what happened. The little creature that was once simply a basic in the pastoral economy became for the Jews (and probably for some other ancient peoples) a symbol not only of gentle helplessness but of ritual sacrifice. And as the Christian community found its faith-language, it claimed its roots in the Hebrew Scriptures. Of course! After all, the first followers of Jesus, including the twelve upon whom the church would be built, were all Jews. So as they read their Scriptures, they saw their Lord not only in the prophecies of the Messiah who was to come but also in the ceremonies and rituals of their faith. For them, becoming followers of Jesus was the natural fulfillment of their pursuit of the faith that had come to them through Abraham and Moses and David.

And so it was that the elements of their traditional worship seemed now to be symbols and shadows of the greater realities they had found in Jesus Christ. This is the basic theme of the New Testament book of Hebrews: "Long ago God spoke to our ancestors in many and various ways by the prophets, but in these last days he has spoken to us by a Son, whom he appointed heir of all things, through whom he also created the worlds" (Hebrews 1:1-2).

And among all those symbols dear to Judaism, perhaps none was as poignant as the lamb that was offered at the Passover night. In their national memory, this lamb had been for each household a substitute for the eldest son. The blood of this lamb had protected the blood of their own lives. Still more, it was the lamb eaten that night that gave strength for the beginning of their journey from slavery to freedom.

But when John the Baptist introduced Jesus, he challenged his audience to see a bigger world and a bigger God than most of them had ever before imagined. Jesus was God's Lamb, but not just for the nation of Israel. He was, John said, "The Lamb of God who takes away the sin *of the world!*" (John 1:2, italics added).

The crucifixion caught this universal theme through the sign Pontius Pilate ordered for Jesus' cross: "Jesus of Nazareth, the King of the Jews . . . and it was written in Hebrew [Aramaic], in Latin, and in Greek" (John 19:19-20)—which were not only the languages spoken throughout Judea but symbolically the language of the Jews and thus of religion, and of government (Latin), and of culture and literature (Greek).

The Gospel of John also focuses our attention on the Passover lamb. As the Friday of the crucifixion wore on and it was necessary that the victims of crucifixion died and were taken down before evening and the beginning of the Sabbath, soldiers broke the legs of the two men crucified with Jesus, thus hastening their death by suffocation. "But when they came to Jesus and saw that he was already dead, they did not break his legs. . . . These things occurred so that the scripture might be fulfilled, 'None of his bones shall be broken'" (John 19:32-33, 36). John is directing us to the instructions given by Moses at the first Passover (Exodus 12:46). Thus we are reminded that Jesus is the Lamb—the ultimate Lamb of which every prior ritual lamb was a sign and symbol.

This insight must have seemed altogether obvious to the first generation of Christians. Thus when Paul wrote to the church at Corinth, he made the kind of sideway reference to Christ as the Lamb in the way one does when one knows that the listener or the reader needs no explanatory data. As the apostle appeals for his people to purify their conduct, he observes in passing, "For our paschal lamb, Christ, has been sacrificed" (1 Corinthians 5:7). The Corinthians were pagan Gentiles, relative novices in any knowledge of the Hebrew Scriptures, yet Paul assumed that they would get his allusion without his enlarging on the matter.

Appropriately, it is in the book of Revelation that the theme of the Lamb comes to its full expression. I say "appropriately" because Revelation is the grand depository of symbols both exotic and ordinary. Further, Revelation gives us the consummation of all things, so if a person or an event is crucial to the plot we can expect them to appear at the consummation.

So here is the statistic. Twenty-nine times in the Revelation Christ is referred to as *the Lamb*. The variety and drama are quite astonishing, but nowhere more than in the first instance. The one receiving the revelation finds himself standing before the throne of God in a blinding setting of worship. The One on the throne holds a scroll "sealed with seven seals"—that is, so securely sealed as to be beyond any ordinary opening. The scroll must be opened, because in it is God's plan for the eternal climax. But who can open such a document as this? The revelator begins to weep, sensing that no one can break the seals.

Then he is reassured. "See, the Lion of the tribe of Judah, the Root of David, has conquered, so that he can open the scroll and its seven seals." And at that moment, as we await the appearance of the Lion, we see "a Lamb, standing as if it had been slaughtered" (Revelation 5:1-6). We detectives have been uncomfortable all through the story of the lamb because so often we've met this word *slaughter*. I could suffer the word *kill*, or even *slay*, but *slaughter* is a word out of the meat industry, *slaughterhouse*. The object of this word is always a creature whose value is simply in the sustenance it gives to others. This is the word that has followed our lamb since the Passover night, even now to the throne of God.

Now we begin to realize that the lamb (or The Lamb) is—contrary to all our usual images—not a pathetic, cuddlesome creature but uniquely powerful. And that the power is in its being slaughtered.

And with this we begin to understand more profoundly what John the Baptizer had in mind when in his inaugural speech he saw need to say no more than, "Here is the Lamb of God who takes away the sin of the world!" It is in the Lamb's being slaughtered at Calvary that the power of sin is utterly broken and redemption is made available to our human race.

But such power brings more than simply comfort. There will come a day, Revelation says, when "the kings of the earth and the magnates and the generals and the rich and the powerful, and everyone, slave and free" will call for protection "from the face of the one seated on the throne and from the wrath of the Lamb" (Revelation 6:15-16).

I promised at the beginning of this story that I would not turn the lamb from victim to perpetrator, and I mean to keep my promise. But anyone who has experienced love at any profound level—parent-child, spouse, friend, advocate-cause—knows that there is no wrath quite so breathtaking as the wrath of sacrificial love. There is a holy wrath in the soldier who throws his body on the grenade to protect his comrades, or the parent who fights fatigue and common sense in endless hours—yes, even endless years—of watching over a sick child. This is the wrath of love, and its ultimate expression is at Golgotha.

The Moravian Church, which has its roots in Count von Zinzendorf and before that in John Hus, has as its symbol a lamb carrying a flag. On the flag is a motto: "Our Lamb has conquered. Let us follow Him."

Our culture reasons that it's a strange people who will follow a lamb. But John the Baptist knew better. And so will the unnumbered multitudes who will gather eventually at the throne of God. They have found that the helpless Lamb of love and sacrifice is the omnipotent Lamb of God's eternal salvation. Behold, the Lamb!

NOTES

1. A Biography of Satan

1. John Milton, *Paradise Lost* (New York: Penguin Books, Signet Classics, 2000), Book I, lines 36-40.

2. Augustine, "Christian Instruction," 3:37, quoted in *Ancient Christian Commentary on Scripture*, Vol X, Old Testament (Downers Grove, Ill.: InterVarsity Press, 2004), 122.

3. Quoted by Fleming Rutledge, *Not Ashamed of the Gospel* (Grand Rapids: Eerdmans Publishing Company, 2007), 200fn.

4. In a lecture, St. Paul Church (Episcopal), Cleveland Heights, Ohio, May 19, 1989.

5. Kathleen Norris, *Amazing Grace: A Vocabulary of Faith* (New York: Riverhead Books, 1998), 46.

6. Rowan Williams, *A Ray of Darkness* (Cambridge, Mass.: Cowley Publications, 1995), 77.

2. Follow the Blood

1. Robert Alter, *The Five Books of Moses* (New York: W. W. Norton & Company, 2004), 944.

2. Ibid., 480-81.

3. Ibid., 557.

4. Translated from the Latin by Paul Gerhardt, 1656. *The United Methodist Hymnal* (Nashville: The United Methodist Publishing House, 1989), no. 286.

5. Thomas Merton, *Praying the Psalms* (Collegeville, Minn.: The Liturgical Press, 1956), 42.

6. Kathleen Norris, *Amazing Grace* (New York: Riverhead Books, 1998), 112, 113.

7. Fleming Rutledge, *Not Ashamed of the Gospel* (Grand Rapids: William B. Eerdmans Publishing Company, 2007) 88.

3. Job Tells His Story

1. Job 5:17.
2. Job 9:32.
3. Job 11:3.
4. Job 16:2.
5. Job 33:15-16.
6. Job 38:3.
7. Job 38:4.
8. Job 38:36.
9. Job 39:1, 5.
10. Job 42:5-6.

5. Who Killed Mother Nature?

1. Rowan Williams, *A Ray of Darkness* (Cambridge, Mass.: Cowley Publications, 1995), 50.
2. Richard John Neuhaus, editor, *The Second One Thousand Years* (Grand Rapids: William B. Eerdmans Publishing Company, 2001), 53-54.
3. *Christian Century*, December 25, 2007, 6.
4. Gerard Manley Hopkins, *"God's Grandeur" and Other Poems* (New York: Dover Publications, 1995), 15.
5. Fleming Rutledge, *Not Ashamed of the Gospel* (Grand Rapids: William B. Eerdmans Publishing Company, 2007), 235.
6. Page 525.

6. Making Do with Remnants

1. Ronald Knox, *The Holy Bible: A Translation from the Latin Vulgate in the Light of the Hebrew and Greek Originals* (London: Burns and Oates, 1995).

7. Christmas Women

1. Alter, *The Five Books of Moses*, 29.

8. Joseph the Dreamer

1. The Random House Dictionary of the English Language (New York: Random House, 1966), 287.

9. The Love Strategy

1. Fleming Rutledge, *Not Ashamed of the Gospel* (Grand Rapids: William B. Eerdmans Publishing Company, 2007), 69.

2. Philip Yancey, *I Was Just Wondering* (Grand Rapids: William B. Eerdmans Publishing Company, 1998), 153-57.

10. Time. And Time Again.

1. William Barclay, *The Gospel of Matthew,* Vol. 1 (Philadelphia: The Westminster Press, 1958), 18.

2. Oscar Cullmann, *Christ and Time* (London: SCM Press, 1952), 42.

11. The Man of Opportunity

1. Robert Alter, *The Five Books of Moses* (New York: W. W. Norton & Company, 2004), 612-13.

2. *The Random House Dictionary of the English Language* (New York: Random House, 1966), 1274.

3. Alter, *The Five Books of Moses,* 614.

DISCUSSION GUIDE FOR *DETECTIVE STORIES FROM THE BIBLE* by J. Ellsworth Kalas

John D. Schroeder

CHAPTER 1
A BIOGRAPHY OF SATAN

Snapshot Summary

This chapter examines the nature of the villain named Satan, his crimes, and his method of operation.

Reflection / Discussion Questions

1. Reflect on / discuss what you hope to gain from your experience of reading and discussing this book.
2. What makes detective stories so interesting? Name some famous detectives from movies, books, or television.
3. What are some of the types of crimes we find detailed in the Bible?
4. Do you see evidence of evil at work in the world today? Explain your answer, and give examples if possible.

5. Reflect on / discuss what the Bible tells us about Satan. How is our view of Satan influenced by nonbiblical literature and tradition?

6. Reflect on / discuss some of the times Jesus encountered Satan and what Jesus had to say about Satan.

7. Share a time when you struggled with Satan or with your views toward Satan. How do you deal with temptation?

8. Reflect on / discuss the author's comment that Satan, "the Adversary," is helpless without our cooperation. How and why is this so?

9. According to Revelation, what will happen to Satan?

10. What help do you believe God provides us in dealing with Satan?

Prayer: *Dear God, thank you for helping us see the nature and the dangers of evil. Help us follow the example of your Son, Jesus, in overcoming Satan's temptations and deception, and in seeing your Truth. Amen.*

CHAPTER 2
FOLLOW THE BLOOD

Snapshot Summary
This chapter examines the symbolism of blood in the Bible, from the first murder to Jesus' blood shed at Calvary.

Reflection / Discussion Questions
1. Name some occasions when you might encounter blood.

2. How would you explain Holy Communion to someone who has never heard of it?

3. Why does the author refer to Communion as a Christian *celebration*?

4. Share why you participate in Communion at your place of worship.
5. Why, according to the author, does the trail of blood in the Bible begin with Cain?
6. Reflect on / discuss reasons primitive peoples involved the use of blood with their religions.
7. Do you agree with the author's assertion that "our sense of the sacredness of blood has diminished" today? Explain your answer.
8. Reflect on / discuss why blood is so prominent in the Hebrew Scriptures.
9. What does the blood of Jesus represent to believers today?
10. What additional insights about following the blood did you receive from reading or discussing this chapter?

Prayer: *Dear God, we thank you that the trail of blood leads to Calvary and to our salvation. Help us read the Bible, believe in Jesus, and know of your love for us. Amen.*

CHAPTER 3
JOB TELLS HIS STORY

Snapshot Summary
This chapter is a mystery story told by Job about a series of disasters in his life and why he continued to trust in God.

Reflection / Discussion Questions
1. What insights into himself does Job reveal in the beginning of his story?
2. What are some of the disasters Job experiences as reported by his messengers?
3. What does Job's wife urge him to do, and what were her motivations for this?

4. Share a time when you faced difficulties and, like Job, wondered why.
5. How did Job's friends react to his circumstances, and what advice did they provide?
6. What do you most admire about Job and why?
7. What does Job's story tell you about God? What does it tell you about facing the problems of life?
8. In what ways is Job's story a mystery?
9. How was Job's situation resolved?
10. What other lessons can we learn from Job's story?

Prayer: *Dear God, thank you for using the story of Job to remind us of your constant love and presence, even in our darkest hours. Help us rely on you in times of trouble. Amen.*

CHAPTER 4
THE ADVANTAGES OF FOURTH PLACE

Snapshot Summary
This chapter gives us clues as to how Judah moved from "fourth place" in life to a remarkable finish as a noted ancestor of Jesus.

Reflection / Discussion Questions
1. "The Advantages of Fourth Place"; why is this both an unusual and a fitting title for this chapter?
2. Give a brief summary of Judah's family background.
3. Why does the author say that Christians have a crucial stake in Judah?
4. How did Judah get his name? What does his name mean?
5. What elements of mystery or the unusual are found in Judah's story?
6. How did Judah help get Joseph to Egypt and further the eternal plan?

7. Give some examples of Judah's less-than-perfect character.
8. Does this chapter suggest personal qualities of Judah that you admire? Explain your answer.
9. What strange words did Jacob speak to his son Judah when Jacob was dying?
10. What lessons can we learn from Judah's story?

Prayer: *Dear God, thank you for reminding us that we all matter and can all make a difference, no matter where we start out in life. Help us serve and love you as we journey through life. Amen.*

CHAPTER 5
WHO KILLED MOTHER NATURE?

Snapshot Summary
This chapter explores the complex relationship between humanity and the earth, and how the scriptures tell us that when we do harm to God's creation, we do harm to ourselves

Reflection / Discussion Questions
1. Share your thoughts on the author's statement, "We humans belong to the earth."
2. How is Cain's murder of his brother, Abel, related to the mystery of "Who Killed Mother Nature"?
3. What are some of our sins, as humanity, against Mother Nature?
4. Who or what else is to blame for the slow killing of Mother Nature? Name some possible suspects.
5. Reflect on / discuss the idea of the sacredness of soil.
6. In what ways might Mother Nature be said to take vengeance against the human race for our attacks against her?
7. According to the author, what did the Apostle Paul have to say about the case of "Who Killed Mother Nature"?
8. God wants us to take good care of the earth; reflect on / discuss what this idea involves.

9. Do you think this "murder" can be prevented? Explain your answer.
10. What new insights into our planet and our relationship with it did you gain from your reading and discussion of this chapter?

Prayer: *Dear God, thank you for warning us again about the dangers our planet—or "Mother Nature"—faces. Help us all come to her rescue. May we cherish this earth, properly care for it, and leave it in better shape for future generations. Amen.*

CHAPTER 6
MAKING DO WITH REMNANTS

Snapshot Summary
This chapter looks at how God uses what others would consider to be cast-offs to create a better world.

Reflection / Discussion Questions
1. Share a time when you made use of leftovers of some sort.
2. In what way was Noah a remnant, and how did God use him?
3. Name some biblical people who could be considered remnants.
4. Explain how God's prophets could be called "specialists in remnanting."
5. What do you admire about the prophet Isaiah? How did he serve God?
6. Reflect on / discuss what Jesus had to say about remnants.
7. In what ways were Jesus' followers and disciples holy remnants?
8. Give some reasons God might prefer to work with remnants.
9. Why is being God's remnant "a precarious calling"?

10. What additional new insights into remnants did you receive from your reading and discussion of this chapter?

Prayer: *Dear God, thank you for using us as remnants and for treasuring each of us. May we work together to create a fabric of love, peace, and faith in this world. Amen.*

CHAPTER 7
CHRISTMAS WOMEN

Snapshot Summary
This chapter searches the Bible for clues in identifying "Christmas women," those who served a role in preparing for the birth of Jesus.

Reflection / Discussion Questions
1. Why, according to the author, do women "have a special claim on Christmas"?
2. How does Eve fit into the story of Christmas women?
3. What is Tamar's story, and how is she a Christmas woman?
4. Reflect on / discuss what is known about Rahab. Why is she remarkable?
5. According to the author, in what way did Ruth "back into" the Christmas story?
6. What do you admire most about Ruth?
7. What role did Bathsheba play in the Christmas story?
8. Describe some of the challenges faced by Christmas women because of their gender and role in society at the time.
9. What special qualities did Mary, the mother of Jesus, possess?
10. In your own life, what role have women played when it comes to Christmas?

Prayer: *Dear God, thank you for all of the women who have played a role in bringing about the Christmas story. Help us remember and honor the important contributions of the Christian women in our lives. Amen.*

CHAPTER 8
JOSEPH THE DREAMER

Snapshot Summary
This chapter examines the lives of two men named Joseph who were dreamers and how their dreams paved the way for the arrival of Jesus.

Reflection / Discussion Questions
1. Share a time when you experienced a coincidence.
2. What do we know about the early life of Joseph the carpenter, the husband of Mary?
3. How were his parents "thinking big" when they named him Joseph?
4. Reflect on / discuss the courtship of Mary and Joseph as outlined by the author.
5. What thoughts do you believe Joseph had when Mary told him she was going to have a child? What were Joseph's options in terms of how to respond?
6. What was Joseph's first dream, and how did it change his mind?
7. What was Joseph's second dream? Reflect on / discuss how Joseph's two dreams influenced the lives of his family.
8. What do you most admire about Joseph?
9. How do dreams connect the two biblical Josephs? What were the results of these dreams?
10. Do you think it was a coincidence that both dreamers were named Joseph? Explain your answer.

Prayer: *Dear God, thank you for coincidences and dreamers, and for the mysterious ways you touch lives in this world. Grant us the ability to move our dreams to reality and to further your kingdom in the process. Amen.*

CHAPTER 9
THE LOVE STRATEGY

Snapshot Summary
This chapter examines the mystery of love, which culminates in God's gift of Christ.

Reflection / Discussion Questions
1. Share some insights you have learned about love through life experiences.
2. In what ways is love a mystery?
3. Reflect on / discuss the beginnings of love and its place in Creation.
4. In what sense might God be referred to as "the jilted lover"?
5. Name some ways in which we reject God and God's love.
6. According to the author, how does God respond to our rejection of God's love?
7. What does the prophet Hosea have to say about the "divine-human mismatch"?
8. How is God's love strategy evidenced in the New Testament?
9. What are some of the ways in which God's love, as the author puts it, "violates common sense"?
10. Reread Romans 5:7-8 and reflect on / discuss this question: how does God "prove his love for us"?

Prayer: *Dear God, thank you for a strategy of love that works and that keeps our world connected to you. Help us love others as you love us. Amen.*

CHAPTER 10
TIME. AND TIME AGAIN.

Snapshot Summary
This chapter explores the mystery of time and traces God's perfect timing through the Bible and beyond.

Reflection / Discussion Questions

1. Share an example of when time really mattered to you.
2. Reflect on / discuss the author's statement that "something in us knows that we are eternal creatures."
3. What does the author of Genesis tell us about God and time?
4. Reflect on / discuss what the Hebrew prophets believed about time.
5. Why was the period when Jesus was born a time of extraordinary expectation?
6. What signs pointed to the birth of Jesus?
7. According to the author, the Apostle Paul saw a "whenness" in the birth of Christ; what does this mean?
8. What insights into time, timing, and God do we get from the writer of the Gospel of John?
9. Explain what is meant by kairos and chronos, and give an example of each.
10. How did your reading and discussion of this chapter help you better understand the mystery of time?

Prayer: *Dear God, thank you for all the time you give us to enjoy life, to enjoy others, and to serve you. Help us make good use of time and not waste a moment. Amen.*

CHAPTER 11
THE MAN OF OPPORTUNITY

Snapshot Summary

This chapter covers the serious nature of sin, the Day of Atonement, and sacrifice as seen through those who took the opportunity to serve God.

Reflection / Discussion Questions

1. How seriously do you think we take sin today as compared to the Israelites of the Old Testament?

2. Reflect on / discuss the Israelites' Day of Atonement and its importance.
3. Give a summary of the Israelites' ritual of the bull and two goats. What did these animals represent?
4. What is the origin and meaning of the term *scapegoat*?
5. What qualities or skills were needed to lead a goat into the wilderness? Why were this person and this task so special?
6. Why does the author refer to the New Testament writers as "sacred detectives"?
7. Reflect on / discuss how Jesus was the ultimate sacrifice, a scapegoat. What does the symbolism of his death mean to you?
8. Share your thoughts about the role of Judas as the man of opportunity in the death of Jesus.
9. Why might Simon of Cyrene also be considered a man of opportunity?
10. What additional thoughts or questions from this chapter would you like to explore?

Prayer: *Dear God, thank you for Christ's loving act of redemption for all of us. May we seek opportunities to serve you and return your love for us. Amen.*

CHAPTER 12
BEHOLD, THE LAMB!

Snapshot Summary
This chapter examines the biblical significance and symbolism of the lamb, from the Old Testament to Revelation.

Reflection / Discussion Questions
1. What does the image of a lamb call to mind for you?
2. How is the lamb portrayed in the Bible? How is the lamb "uniquely powerful" and not weak?

3. According to the author, what role might a lamb have played in the Garden of Eden?
4. What are your thoughts on the story of Abraham and his son Isaac as it relates to this chapter?
5. Briefly describe the significance of the lamb in the observance of Passover.
6. Reflect on / discuss John the Baptist's introduction of Jesus.
7. Explain how the theme of the lamb comes to full expression in the book of Revelation.
8. How are we reminded throughout the Bible that Jesus is the ultimate Lamb?
9. What additional thoughts or questions from this chapter would you like to explore?
10. Share what you learned from your reading and discussion of this book.

Prayer: *Dear God, thank you for this opportunity to be a detective and to examine your Word and your truth as found in the Bible. Bless us as we seek new ways to serve you and to let others know of your love. Amen.*